The Astrology of Indigos, Everyday Solutions to Spiritual Difficulties

Mary English

Published by Mary English, 2019.

THE ASTROLOGY OF INDIGOS, EVERYDAY SOLUTIONS TO SPIRITUAL DIFFICULTIES

First edition. April 14, 2019.

ISBN: 978-1393655954

Written by Mary English.

Also by Mary English

The Astrology of Lovers, How Astrology Can Help You Love Better
The Astrology of Indigos, Everyday Solutions to Spiritual Difficulties

This book is dedicated to my son SG,

May Your Life be Blessed with Love and Light

The Astrology of Indigos
Everyday Solutions to Spiritual Difficulties
Understanding the Alignment of Outer Planets and Cluster Charts
Mary English

First published by Hensley Healing Publishing October 2013

Contents

Also by Mary English

6 Easy Steps in Astrology

How to Survive a Pisces (O-Books)

How to Bond with an Aquarius (O-Books)

How to Cheer up a Capricorn (O-Books)

How to Believe in a Sagittarius (O-Books)

How to Win the Trust of a Scorpio (Dodona Books)

How to Love a Libra (Dodona Books)

How to Soothe a Virgo (Dodona Books)

How to Lavish a Leo (Dodona Books)

How to Care for a Cancer (Dodona Books)

How to Listen to a Gemini (Dodona Books)

How to Satisfy a Taurus (Dodona Books)

How to Appreciate an Aries (Dodona Books)

The Astrology of Lovers

A Little at a Time, Homeopathy for You and Those You Love (Ayni Books part of John Hunt Publishing) where I live and was drawn to buy a book called 'The Indigo Children' by Jan Tober and Lee Carroll.

The book described so accurately this particular boy and his problems, that I then bought 'The Care and Feeding of Indigo Children' by Doreen Virtue, so I could offer his Mum some hope and explain that this boy isn't a challenge, the system looking after him is.

Then I compared his chart to others in my collection and noticed a striking similarity with certain children's charts I had treated recently and some I had treated quite a few years before. Then another boy from the first boy's class was brought to me and *his* chart had the same configuration and so did my son's, who was also in the class. In fact over 10 children in this year all had similar charts. This set me on a mission that still intrigues me to this day.

Indigo Research

Later that year I decided to do a small amount of personal research and posted some details on an Indigo website asking for birth data. The site I used was only visited by people interested in Indigos, and I decided to use the data from 100 people. After 100 people had given me their birth data, I published, only on my own website the results. Of the 100 people, 95 of them had one-sided charts.

I thought this was reasonably significant so I wanted other astrologers and Indigos to know, that there was something happening astrologically when they were born.

I will explain more about Astrology in Chapter 1.

Since I published my article in 2004, it has been read by over 100,000 people and is still being read at a rate of about 10,000 people a year. When I first published it though, it was copied onto a number of sites, (without my permission) so I don't have completely accurate figures about its readership. I only have the stats from my own site, so those figures might be larger. I have kept the article there, so it can be read by anyone wanting to know about the Astrology of Indigos.

I have given talks about the Astrology of Indigos and my article was published in the Astrological Association of Great Britain's journal.

I thought maybe, over the years, the phenomena would die down but I'm still contacted by numbers of people every week asking about their charts and about Indigos and have given advice and help to the people that contact me after reading the article.

This book has been written to expand on that article and to give more information about how Astrology *reflects* our experience on planet earth and *explains* the Astrology of the Indigo phenomenon.

Mary English, Bath May 2013

Chapter 1

What is Astrology?

Astrology has a very ancient history. As long as there have been humans on the planet, there has been a search to make sense out of chaos and to add meaning to our lives.

The first astrologers were the Babylonians. They lived in what is now called Iraq, way before the birth of Christ.

A Brief History of Astrology

As Historian Christopher McIntosh tells us:

Astrology dates back to our earliest records of human learning. It is the precursor of astronomy as for many years they were one science. The mainstream of astrology has its source in an area which was also the beginning of Western civilisation: the Middle East.

Here man laid down his hunting weapons, abandoned the nomadic life-style, and settled down with plough and scythe to develop an agricultural society. This settled society brought more leisure and a disciplined government and with that came organised religion with temples and priests. 1.

Ancient Priests

The earliest references to astrology lie with the Babylonians in 2000 BC. The priests of the kingdom of Babylonia, the present day Iraq, made the discovery, which set the pattern for the development of astronomy and the zodiacal system of astrology that we know today. For generations they methodically observed and recorded the movements of the heavenly bodies. Finally, they discovered, by careful calculation that in addition to the Sun and the Moon, five other visible planets moved in established routes through the sky.

These were the planets that we now call Mercury, Venus, Mars, Jupiter and Saturn.

These priests lived very isolated lives in monasteries usually near to towers called ziggurats from which they could observe the night sky. One major advantage of living next to the Persian Gulf was the extremely clear skies and they managed to make their calculations without telescopes or any complicated equipment. Every day they observed the movements of the planets and noted down any corresponding earthly phenomena from floods to rebellions. Very early on they came to the conclusion that the laws that governed the movements of the stars and planets also governed events on Earth.

Gods

Early on the stars and planets were regarded as being actual gods. Later, as their religion became more sophisticated, the two ideas were separated and the belief developed that the god 'ruled' the corresponding planet. Gradually, a highly complex system was built up in which each planet had a particular set of properties ascribed to it. This system was developed partly through the reports of the priests and partly though the natural characteristics of the planets. Mars was seen to be red in colour and was therefore identified with the god Nergal, the fiery god of war and destruction. Venus was the most prominent in the morning, giving birth as it were, to the day. She therefore became the planet associated with the female qualities of love and gentleness, as well as with the function of procreation. At first their observations only centred around their community but as time went on, between 600 and 300 BC this system became more precise and during this period individual horoscopes were cast.

Astrology Today

Fast forward to today where astrology is a mixture of light relief or firm belief and hopes for the future and is practiced in every country in the world. What I will be discussing here is western astrology. Each system is based on how the planets are 'viewed' from our place on earth.

The belief is: "As Above, So Below". That we are all part of the same wonderful cosmos, we all exist because of each other, not in spite of, and therefore are influenced by and are of influence to, all parts of our 'world'.

An Astrological Birth chart is based on a map of the heavens on the day, time and location of someone's birth. The map is constructed by calculating the position of the various planets in the sky. This map or birth chart is like your finger-prints.

It never changes. People get a bit confused about astrology and think the birth chart 'predicts' everything to do with someone's life. That's not actually true. The birth chart illustrates what sort of character you are, your potential. What happens in your life (in my opinion) is not fated, more the result of choices you make. The predictive bit of astrology is determined by calculating where the planets will be in the future in relation to where they were when you were born. A sort of astral comparison.

Important Notes

Planet: A celestial body that orbits around the Sun.

Star: With the exception of the Moon and the planets, every fixed point of light in the sky is a star, including the Sun. However in astrology we use the term 'planet' for all the bits we use. So if you catch me calling the Sun a planet, that is an astrological term, not one used in astronomy.

Your Chart of the Heavens

If you imagine that the centre of a birth chart is the earth, the map is made up of where each planet was, in each segment of the sky, around us in the cosmos.

We use a circle to plot the planet positions, which is now made 100% easier, by using computer programmes. In the 'old days' the cycles of the movements and placements of the planets were made by educated men and the information kept in a book called an Ephemeris. Nowadays, all you need to do is use a good computer programme or the wonderful free Swiss resource http://www.astro.com

If you go to their website and make an account, you can create your own chart. I do recommend using the chart-making system called Equal House. After you've created your account, go to the page marked free horoscopes and scroll down until you see Extended Chart Selection. Click on this and you'll now be on a page with lots of options. This is the page Astrologers use to make their charts personal and the way they like them as there are at least 5 chart systems.

Chart Systems

There are numerous way to calculate a chart. I use the system called Equal House as it is the oldest system and I think if it isn't broken don't fix it! The other systems were introduced by various different blokes over the years and are called things like Placidus (after the man that used it), Koch (ditto) Regiomontanus. Most computer programmes are automatically set to Placidus which makes your chart look lop-sided and uneven. Unfortunately astro.com is set to this system and you won't see the correct shape of a chart using it.

We're now going to make your chart using Equal House.

On this page, scroll to data and choose equal house, ignore all the others....

Now click the red button: 'make chart' and bingo! Your chart will appear on the next page as equal house and all your houses, or segments of your chart will be of equal size = 30 degrees.

You will need three pieces of information to make your chart: your date of birth, your time of birth, and your location of birth.

We are going to use the imaginary chart of someone called Ben who was born on 15 September 1980, at 4 PM in London England.

Each birth chart or horoscope includes the 10 planets: The Sun, the Moon, Mercury, Venus, Mars, Jupiter, Saturn, Uranus, Neptune and Pluto. The last three weren't discovered by the Babylonians as telescopes hadn't been invented and they were far too distant in space to be seen with the naked eye but knowledge of their existence is vital to understand Indigos. Each planet represents a different part of the psyche.

The most important parts of a chart for a beginner are the Ascendant, the sign of the Sun and the sign of the Moon. In my How to Survive the Zodiac series of books I explain what are the meanings of each house.

The Ascendant

How you came into the world

The Ascendant is determinded by the actual *time* of birth, so you need to know the accurate time to get the correct Ascendant because it changes sign every two hours. So someone born at 10am will have a different Ascendant from someone born at 12pm. In astrology we classify the Ascendant as being the ouside part of you, the bit that people meet first. The image we want people to see, in fact the image people *will* see. Your Ascendant is what you display at a party, or to your parents, or when you're under pressure. It's the coat you wear, the glasses you see the world through, how you viewed the world when you came into it. Your beginning. As you were being born, *the* most important part of your chart was in a sign signifying how you 'came into the world'. It could be in the sign of Virgo making you discriminating, analytical and prone to wanting to categorise things. Or it could be in the sign of Cancer, wanting to 'feel at home' , loving Mum, wanting protection and financial security. Each sign has a different meaning. So you could be a Leo = firey, jolly, dramatic with a Capricorn Ascendant = shy, ambitious, determinded.

Or maybe you were born around 6am, then your Ascendant and your Sun sign will be probabally in the same sign. Taking into account your Ascendant makes your chart individual to you and far more personalised than just knowing your Sun sign....

The Sun

Rules who you are

The Sun represents who you are. The ego. That which identifies you. Most people know what Sun sign they are, even if they don't know anything else about astrology. In a birth chart the sign and location (house placement) of the Sun describes how you will tackle life. Will you be fearless or timid, creative or sporty? It also describes what you will find interesting and how you will express your personality. As the Sun goes through each sign of the Zodiac, it corresponds with the seasons, so someone who was born in December (above the equator) will have been born in the Winter.

From our viewpoint on Earth, it looks as if the Sun moves from one part of the sky to another as the seasons progress, and it was this movement that the Babylonians plotted.

The Sun is a star and a life-giving one at that. Without it our lives would be bleak and cold. In astrology we view the Sun as telling us what our motivation is, what our sense of self is and how we are created. The main focus of our personality.

Looking at it in a very simplistic manner, someone born during the month of August is likely to be a bit more 'sunny' than someone born in the depths of Winter.

Most people resonate with the standard descriptions of their Sun sign. There is a big difference between a Capricorn and a Leo! The sign of the Sun changes every 30 days or so and doesn't quite correspond to the months of the year as they are based on maths not on the cycle of the Sun.

The general accepted dates are :
Aries 21 March - 20 April
Taurus 21 April - 21 May
Gemini 22 May - 21 June
Cancer 22 June- 22 July
Leo 23 July – 23 August
Virgo 24 August - 22 September
Libra 23 September – 23 October

Scorpio 24 October – 22 November
Sagittarius 23 November – 21 December
Capricorn 22 December – 20 January
Aquarius 21 January – 18 February
Pisces 19 February – 20 March

No Such Thing as a Cusp

If you were born on the day when the Sun was changing sign, check with astro.com to find out, once and for all, exactly what sign you are as there is no such thing as a cusp. You are either one sign or another, you can't be both!

The Moon

Rules the emotions and instincts

The Moon in Astrology represents how we feel about things. If the Sun is who we are, and the Ascendant is how we project ourselves, then the Moon is how we respond emotionally to things. In reality the Moon reflects the light of the Sun, so we say it represents how we are emotionally, subconciously. As you may know the Moon affects the tides and the water on Earth, and our emotions are generally quite watery things!

The sign of your Moon might be completely different to the sign of your Sun. This is because the Moon changes sign approximately every two days. This can make your life more complicated until you get to grips with those different signs and energies. Someone with a Fire sign Sun and a Water sign Moon might find it harder to allow their emotions to flow. There could be a conflict between wanting something and being emotionally settled with it.

The Birth Chart

When you've created your chart, it might look like gobbledeegook at first glance. Don't get put off by all the weird symbols and the coloured lines going through it. This is just an international astrological language that anyone from any country in the world can interpret.

If you knew nothing about Astrology before you chose this book, you might have thought 'but I'm a Scorpio, why would I need to know about all the other signs?'

We have ALL the signs in all of our charts. Our Sun sign might be one sign but as there are 10 planets it's unlikely that we'll have all our planets in all of the signs. Even if our planets are in only a few signs, our houses will contain the missing signs and every month the Moon will transit through them, and over your life-time all the other planets will too.

Some move faster than others, the Moon being the fastest.

This is what your birth chart (or natal chart as they call it in the USA) will show you: which bits are in which signs.

Your chart, instead of having the signs Aries to Pisces written on them, will have these symbols for each sign. We call them glyphs.

The Signs and Their Symbols

Aries

Here we have the Ram's horns, ready to 'push' you forward.

Taurus

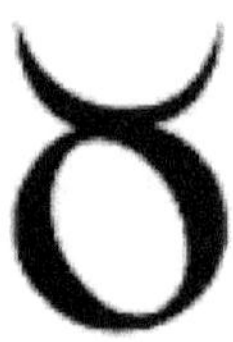

In ancient times, the cattle had curly horns, so the symbol for the bull is again the horns.

Gemini

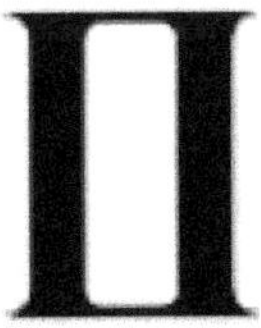

As Gemini is the twins, the glyph symbol has two parts joined at the top and bottom.

Cancer

The glyph for Cancer represents the nurturing breasts.

Leo

The Lion's mane makes the symbol for Leo.

Virgo

The symbol for Virgo looks like a capital M with its tail curled inwards (not to be confused with Scorpio's symbol that is similar but the tail points outwards and has a sting on the end!) It's said to represent the intestines, as this is the area of the body 'ruled' by Virgo.

Libra

The Libra scales of justice are represented in their symbol and are the only inanimate object in the Zodiac.

Scorpio

The symbol for Scorpio is the capital M again (like Virgo) and has a tail with a pointy end, representing the sting of the scorpion.

Sagittarius

Nice easy one to remember as the arrow, as Sagittarius is the archer.

Capricorn

I have no idea what this symbol is supposed to represent, it's a strange shape. As Capricorn is the sea-goat, one bit could be the horns, one the sea-tail but don't quote me!

Aquarius

Aquarius is the water *carrier*, not a water *sign*. It's actually an Air sign and the two waves represent the flowing of the waters of knowledge.

Pisces

Another double-bodied Sun sign, the symbol for Pisces represents the two fishes swimming in opposite directions. One upstream, the other downstream, joined by their tails.

The Planets

It will also have symbols for each planet.

Here are the planets:

Sun

This is the circle of life with the spot in the centre representing our 'self'

Moon

As you might expect the symbol for the Moon looks like the crescent Moon. An easy one to remember

Mercury

☿

Mercury is the messenger and his symbol looks like a cross with a circle hat and a curve on top. These represent the circle of life, the cross of directions, east west south north and the curly hat is how we receive information

Venus

♀

This symbol looks like the ones used for 'female', which hasn't changed in thousands of years

Mars

♂

Again an ancient symbol meaning 'male'.

Jupiter

I think this looks like the number 4

Saturn

Looks like a small h with a cross on top

Uranus

Is a more modern symbol and has the circle of life with what looks like an antennae on top that can receive electricity, bit like the old TV aerial as Uranus governs electricity and all things that happen suddenly.

Neptune

This symbol looks like the trident that Neptune the Water God holds in his hand

Pluto

Has 2 symbols,one is nice and easy to remember as it looks like a capital P, the other looks like the Mercury symbol but it has the circle on top.

Planets in Signs

If you are in a bit of a rush you can skip all of this information by looking at the grid at the bottom left-hand section of your horoscope.

Name: ♂ Ben astro-of-ind born on Mo., 15 September 1980 in London, ENG (UK) 0w10, 51n30	Time: 4:00 p.m. Univ.Time: 15:00 Sid. Time: 14:38:14	ASTRO DIENST www.astro.com Type: 2.GW 0.0-1 26-Aug-2013

Natal Chart (Method: Web Style / equal)
Sun sign: Virgo
Ascendant: Capricorn

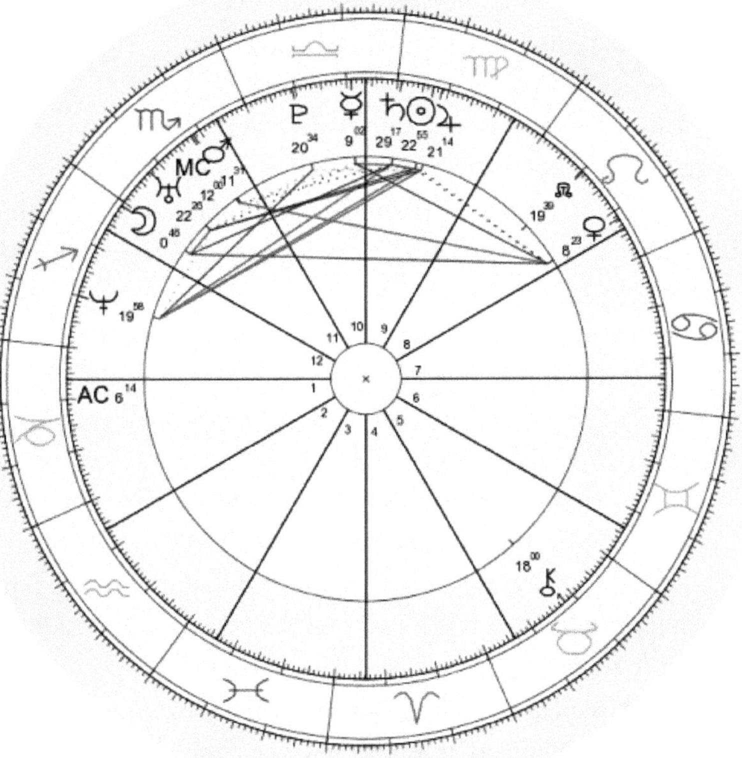

☉ Sun	22 Vir 54'43"
☽ Moon	0 Sag 46'29"
☿ Mercury	9 Lib 2' 0"
♀ Venus	8 Leo 23'25"
♂ Mars	11 Sco 30'57"
♃ Jupiter	21 Vir 14' 7"
♄ Saturn	29 Vir 16'41"
♅ Uranus	22 Sco 26' 15"
♆ Neptune	19 Sag 57'42"
♇ Pluto	20 Lib 33'46"
☊ True Node	19 Leo 39' 9"
⚷ Chiron	17 Tau 59'58"r

AC: 6 Cap 13'58"	2: 6 Aqu 14'	3: 6 Pis 14'
MC: 11 Sco 59'49"	11: 6 Sco 14'	12: 6 Sag 14'

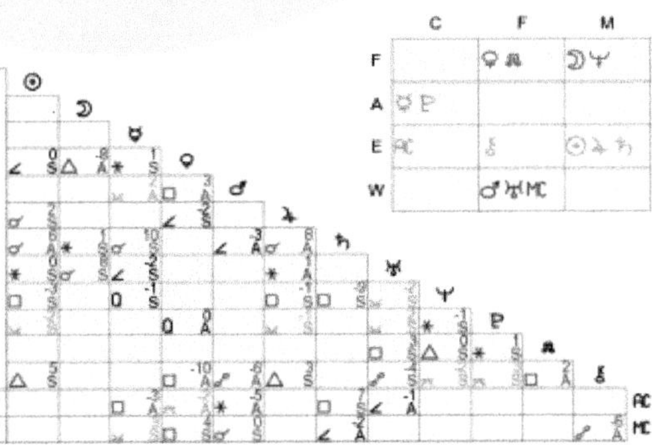

Here will be recorded all the planets in your chart and the signs each one is in, in English or whatever language your site/programme is set to.

Here's our example info for Ben who was born on the 15th September 1980, at 4pm in London, England.

It says O Sun 22 Vir 54' 43"

This translates into someone whose Sun is in the sign of Virgo at 22 degrees, 54 minutes and 43 seconds.

Each sign of the Zodiac in the circle of the birth chart is mathematically 30 degrees, and as there are 12 signs, we end up with 360 degrees.

So, if your Sun is 22 degrees into Virgo, you are just over 2/3rds of the way through that sign.

Don't worry too much about all the maths, all you need to do is find out the *sign* of each planet.

In our example chart, Ben has his Sun in the sign of Virgo, his Moon in Sagittarius, his Mercury in Libra and so on....

At the bottom of the grid it will say the sign of the Ascendant and it's abbreviated to the initials AC, and in Ben's case is 6 Cap 13' 58", and in simple terms it's in the sign of Capricorn.

There is plenty of free information on wwwastro.com which I highly recommend as it is the most accurate, free resource on the Internet.

I've covered, briefly, some starter information about astrology and a few points about the birth chart or horoscope.

Now we will look at what an Indigo actually is...

Chapter 2

What is/are Indigos?

The Indigo concept has quite a chequered history. It originated in the late 1970s and was a term used by a lady called Nancy Anne Tappe. She lived in the USA and had a condition called synaesthesia. This is when the body's sensory systems are entangled and people see and hear things differently. For instance somebody might find that numbers have different tastes, or that letters of the alphabet have different colours. Nancy's synaesthesia meant that she saw colours emanating from people. A bit like seeing auras. But Nancy's condition meant she saw people's life purpose as a colour.

In 1982 she wrote a book called Understanding your Life Thru Color and in it she wrote that she considered herself to 'be' the colour yellow.

She spent her early life living with her grandmother who was of Scottish descent and had what is called "second sight". Her siblings thought she and her grandmother were strange:

"I mean, I saw people all around them and they didn't see anyone. Someone would die and be standing right beside them. They would talk about that person as if they were not there and could never be again. Now to me that was strange!!"

When Nancy was 27 she attended a yoga class and during a candle meditation discovered that the colour she saw around people was called an aura:

"Altered consciousness? I had always seen them. Was I always altered? What was normal to others? Didn't everyone see those bright beautiful colours that made even the worst things not quite so bad? I didn't understand. They really and truly were not seeing them? How dull their worlds must look without colour, other than what is in dyes and pigment. What a pity! And I'm strange?"

Curse Becomes a Gift

Her yoga instructor said: "Nancy, you should develop your gift. It is beautiful." *"Suddenly"*, said Nancy, *"my curse is now a gift"...*

Nancy spent the remaining years of her life working with clients, helping them by 'reading' their life colours.

In her book, she mentions that a new colour had 'come in' at the end of the 1970's and 'replaced' Magenta. That colour was Indigo.

Life Colours

Keeping in mind that in Nancy's world, everyone has different colours surrounding them, she classified each person with certain characteristics, according to 'their' colours.

She learned what each colour signified, and how to interpret each colour combination.

In their later book, Indigo Storm, written a few years before Nancy died, her friend Kathy explained how Nancy saw between nine and thirteen colours around a person at all times. She believed that over a lifetime the colours would change *'in width and intensity, depending on the environment and circumstances of that person's life. One colour, however, remains the same throughout the person's life.'*

Nancy called it the 'cradle to grave' colour or 'life colour' and it would reveal (to her) the focus of that person's life. 6

This colour is the colour we are talking about when we're talking about Indigos. They might have auras that are a mix of other colours, but their predominant Life Colour is Indigo.

The Indigo Children Concept Becomes a Book

Lee Carroll and Jan Tober picked up the idea and expanded it in their book 'The Indigo Children.'

They work in the Mind, Body and Spirit field and channel an entity called Kyron. Until their book was written, there was no mention of Indigos or Indigo children, other than in Nancy's book Understanding your Life Thru Color, so we do have to credit them with bringing the idea forward. We also have to credit Nancy for 'seeing' this new colour first.

Now all of this could quite easily be discounted if it weren't for the astrology behind it.

As I explained in the introduction, the premise is that Indigos are 'new' and 'different'. Well actually, astrologically, they are! They were born during a planetary happening, that won't happen again for another 170 years.

And the timing of their 'discovery' as well as their births was also astrologically significant. The book was published in May 1999 when Uranus and Neptune were conjunct in Aquarius.

As an Astrologer I always check the dates that 'things' happen as they are as interesting as the 'thing' observed is.

Here is what John Hare, a writer for an Astrology programme called Zodiac (that I use) wrote in 1997

CHANGE & INNOVATION

Uranus in Aquarius

Astrologically this is a good place for Uranus since it rules the sign, meaning that all of Uranus's eccentricity is supported and encouraged by Aquarian energy. This placement implies that your generation is all about acceptance of individuality, of the discovery that freedom comes from just being who you are, an issue that the more optimistic of us feel has been one of the big themes of the 20th C. It could be a big theme of the 21st too, since Uranus is in Aquarius during the late 1990's, as I write this, and should be casting its influence over the generation being born now.

SPIRITUALITY & INTUITION

Neptune in Aquarius

1998-2010. Looking a little into the future now - but then, this is astrology so we're allowed to. This placement of Neptune is slightly contradictory in one astrological sense: - it -places the central Neptunian concept of unity and unifying next to the central Aquarian urge for independence. Thus we get a desire to unify through independence. One feels that, born with this placement, you are going to be pulled between a complicated path to genuine unity - the unity of the real you, and a feeling that the two goals are irreconcilable.

Sparked An Interest

The Indigo idea was not just a passing fad. It sparked the interest in the over half a million people that bought the Indigo Children book and read it in over 14 different languages.

According to Google Trends (a search analysis) 2005 was the peak of Indigo Children searches.

These are search terms now:

The Indigo Children

Crystal Children

Indigo Children Test

Indigo Children Characteristics

Indigo Adults

On my website searches were/are:

Indigo children symbol

Indigo children years of birth

How to identify indigo children

An Indigo child's birth chart

Being born with an old soul

Clustered planets in natal chart

Indigo children birth years

Why indigo has to be born after 1978

Natal charts of star seeds

A Sense of Knowing

Lee and Jan made a list of certain attributes that they thought the Indigos possessed. The most striking of all being that they 'come into the world with a sense of knowing'.

They also listed these other characteristics that 'determine' an Indigo child:

1) They come into the world with a feeling of royalty.

2) They have a feeling of deserving to be here.

3) Self-worth is not a big issue.

4) They have difficulty with authority by ritual or without explanation.

5) They simply will not do certain things.

6) They get frustrated with systems that don't require creative thought.

7) They often see better ways of doing things.

8) School is often difficult for them and they can seem antisocial.

9) They will not respond to guilt-trip discipline.

10) They are not shy about letting you know what they need.

I'd agree with these ideas as most of the Indigos that I work with, do have a deeper sense of themselves. They certainly know 'who' they are. Maybe they are also a little more self-assured, less likely to need instruction, more needing guidance and they enjoy helping themselves, or being self-taught much more than *being* taught.

Wikipedia

Over the years I have kept an eye on the Wikipedia page for Indigo children. Unfortunately it doesn't mention anything about Astrology or the spiritual side of Indigos and a lot of visitors who go there 'looking for answers' come away no better informed than they were before. What I find interesting is the editors of the article are more interested in recording the negative side of Indigos, saying that the whole thing was a money making exercise. Maybe some of it was. Maybe it wasn't. What Indigos really need is an answer to 'why am I here, at this time, in this life?' ...not lots of critical arguments about if Indigos exist. Of course they do! Some of them wrote/argued about/edited the page and others are *reading* the Wikipedia page!

It's those questions I hope to answer for you, or at least show you how you can find an answer.

Being Psychic

Indigos are blessed with more psychic ability than their parents or teachers. It's hard-wired into their psyche. But unlike their parents or teachers, they don't find this unusual. They instinctively know when 'things' are right ... or wrong. If you're wondering why this is the case, read on about Neptune (planet of psychic ability) and Uranus (planet of sudden happenings and freedom).

Every person has a psychic ability, just the same as everyone can dream but not everyone can remember their dreams. It's the same way with psychic ability. We're born with it, use it when we're younger, then forget. Most Indigos haven't forgotten and they continue to use their psychic ability when they're grown. They take it for granted that it exists.

Here we have Karen, an Indigo that lives in Mississippi and is a Virgo.

"My experience of that moment when you have a 'Just Knowing' incident at the right time.

The more I work on myself as a person mentally and spiritually the more phenomena I am experiencing!

Football season is starting off so I head up to Ole Miss to celebrate my boyfriend and my birthday. (Today is my birthday yesterday was his!)

As I'm up in this really relaxed sports bar, we were watching an intense game on TV Ole Miss vs. Van(derbilt). It was a really close game in the 4th quarter but Van scored a touch down at 1:30 that just sealed the victory for the college. I could greatly feel the sheer disappointment in everybody in the room. But, I told my boyfriend's brother not to worry because Ole Miss will definitely score a touch down within the last minute and thirty seconds. He said there was no way that it was going to happen.

I told him to watch. So he roughed it out and sure enough, Ole scored the touch down and won the game! Everybody was so psyched but even more psyched that I was able to call so easily with confidence. They asked me how did I know, I told them I just knew it was going to happen.

I love it! Haha!"

Here is Victoria, a Sagittarius

"Hi, my name is Victoria. For a while I was told I was a indigo child so about 2 years ago I started studying a lot, figuring out who I am and to be honest I still don't know lol.

I'm now seeing patterns in the air. I can play with energy, manifest it, pull energy strings, make orbs. I feel as if I'm an energy worker. Just don't know how to use this. It's so amazing!"

Sometimes their psychic ability isn't always a fun experience.

Zara is having problems with what she calls her 'flow'.

"I cannot control my psychic flow. My flow of energy is out of my control, sometimes I'm scared of my own pencil at school, or I'm crying because I don't have the strength to lift myself off of the floor, other times I get headaches, and my head feels dry and empty, and other times I just seem like a normal 14 year old girl. I don't know what to do. I want my energy channel to be open, but I don't want it to flood over me, like it has before."

Being in This world, But Not of This World

Elena is a 21-year-old Gemini, and lives in Vilnius in Lithuania. She was at college studying journalism and also has singing lessons privately. She comes from a small family and works hard at her studies. She and I have been communicating by email for a few years now. She knows she's an Indigo and I feel she's a perfect example of an Indigo life well-lived.

Elena:

"Have you ever had a dream, that you were so sure was real? What if you were unable to wake from that dream? How would you know the difference between the dream world and the real world?" – Morpheus

asked Neo in "The Matrix". For these almost two weeks I felt like I was somewhere in between the real world and the dream world. And now I am back to the planet. This time for sure. Today around 3.30pm I suddenly felt like I have woken up. Not like when you wake up gradually but when you suddenly open your eyes and realize that "it was just a dream". I even asked myself a few times have I been at my singing lesson already or was it another dream? And it still seems blurry when I try to remember the lesson, as if I would be trying to remember a dream. If it wasn't past 3 and I wasn't in a bus, I'd think I had another dream and it's time to get up now."

So I asked her:

Does it feel good or bad to be back on earth?

...and she replied:

'It's neither good or bad. It's nothing unusual. It happens naturally for me occasionally, periods when I'm somewhere "out there", they eventually end and I am "back to earth". But it was never that sudden and the period was usually no longer than a few days. I have always felt like I am walking the line between the two worlds, sometimes I am more in this one, sometimes in the other. It's like living two separate lives in rotation. I can't state any of them as better. Only this time everything was much more intense than usual.'

This is something that Indigos do a lot. They spend periods of time not being 'in their bodies'. I'm not too sure why this is, maybe it's because they haven't quite got the hang of being a human, or they're regressing back to a previous life, or they still feel as if they're up there with the fairies and the angels, where nothing hurts and they're returned to 'The Source'. Spending time out of your body is OK but only for short amounts of time, because if you do it too much, when you do return, you can come back with quite a clunk.

However, their ability to look at life in a different way and reveal easier solutions to problems, makes Indigos such a valuable generation, it's so sad how they've been labelled as having ADD and being 'problem' children.

Zeitgeist and The Venus Project

Elena self-studies but look at what she's studying! It's life-changing material

'I am now doing a lot of work for the Zeitgeist movement Lithuanian chapter and I've wanted to write an article for a long time to the website about human evolution. When I didn't know anything about the Zeitgeist movement or the Venus project and a friend tried to explain it to me and tried to get me to watch the movie... And I was so interested in the topic of the indigo children, and I tried to explain that to him... Eventually we got to the point where while he was talking about a new civilization and I was talking about the new generation he was the one to say "Hey, those people you're talking about would be the perfect citizens of that new world". That's when I saw the movies, got into the idea and realized it all fits and it all finally makes sense now! The point is - I know it, he knows it, maybe a few more people know it, but most don't. And most people still raise questions like "but you can't change the people", "but what about human nature" and all else that falls into that category and is oh so obvious already to me. So I was carrying this idea in my head for over a year now, and as more and more questions arise I have more and more motivation to put it into an article so that more people would get the idea of how it is all connected and how the world is already on the natural path towards the goal of the Venus project.'

Zeitgeist was a self-produced film released on YouTube that explained how the monetary systems and governments actually 'work'. It doesn't make easy watching as some of it is rather depressing and violent but the film-maker, a chap called Peter Joseph is making the point not to trust governments and institutions, something I'm in complete agreement with.

Mr Joseph (which isn't his real name) was born just as the Indigo phenomena began at the end of the 1970s, so I expect he's an Indigo too but there is no way of discovering his birth data... yet...

Elena then has a psychic insight regarding a relative that had died before she was born.

"I would think I'm developing some form of insanity if it was the first unusual encounter with something "impossible". Some years ago I had a dream of a woman who came into our house and acted like she's at home which annoyed me and when I asked her who she is, she said she's a distant relative that I don't know. The day after I told my mother about it and her eyes widened in surprise when I described the woman in detail. After a while when we were visiting my grandfather, she got him to take out some old family albums, found a picture of a woman and showed it to me. I recognized her immediately. Apparently she was a relative, she was married to my mother's uncle, but she died before I was even born. And I couldn't blame it on "maybe I've seen the picture in that album before", because when I described how she was dressed in my dream and what her hair looked like, my mother told me that was exactly how she looked in the coffin, THAT I could not possibly know in such detail. After that close encounter with the beyond, I don't rush to credit things to "insanity"... Could be real after all. Similar things happened more than once, only this is the one particular that has absolutely no "logical" explanation. Maybe I did live in Ancient Egypt around the times of Cleopatra in one of my past lives, that would certainly explain my extreme interest in the period. Although my mother used to say every child goes through that "I love Ancient Egypt" phase. But in my case, the "phase" never really ended :)"

Spiritual Connection

Indigos need to have some sort of spiritual connection. They want to know how to connect with 'the divine' or the divinity within themselves. It's a permanent quest.

Kristina is an Aries and was born in Belarus. She tells us about her first experience of finding spiritual guidance.

"I was 15 and was on the vacation with my Mum and Brother at my Grandmother's in Belarus. She used to go to the library which was close to her house and when my Mum was coming around, she used to help my Granny to pick the books, newsletters and magazines. One day I decided to go to the library together with my Mum (before going there I asked my Mum to pick something on psychology for me, but she advised me to go with her and pick something which I would like. So I went with her).

We came to the library and the librarian gave me a strange look when I asked about psychology books and said that they have nothing on psychology but I might want to go to another room and to check one bottom shelf. So I did that and the first book I picked was a green book, which was called "The light source of love" by Luule Viilma.

Though the book was quite thick, I read it in one week. I was impressed and amazed. I have never read anything like this before but somehow I had a feeling that the things which were written in the book were very well known by me, but forgotten. I had a feeling in my heart, that the things, which the book was about, were all true. I just knew that.

The book I read was about the source of love, forgiveness and on the other side - about the sources of diseases. It was about the connection of our thoughts, behaviour, deep fears and unforgiveness from one side, and our physical body (as the material part of all our bodies). So, first is our perception, our attitude, our fears and unforgiveness and then it leads to health problems.

She tells that by forgiving ourselves we can cure our bodies. She gives examples of what we should do (or rather - say) to cure our diseases.

I found this book very interesting and decided to make a research about Luule and her books. I found even more books and read them. They were very inspiring for me,

I just loved them. They are very wise and I had a feeling that they teach about things which are basic in life of all people. They are based on kindness, love and forgiveness and when I was reading them, I felt how they were opening my heart and I felt my heart responding to the books."

In this short example, Kristina tells us how important discovering the 'Light Source of Love' was from her.

Just read that title again.

Doesn't it make you want to read it?

Wouldn't you want to know what it was all about?

Wouldn't you want to know about why we get ill, or how our thoughts are connected to our bodies?

Mind, Body, Spirit

I write in what's called the Mind, Body, and Spirit category ... because I know there is a connection between the mind and the body. How couldn't there be? They have to be connected and just as our bodies are connected to our minds, our minds are connected to other minds.

There definitely is a thing called 'group thought'. It's not always positive though, but humans all have the same needs: to be fed, safe, loved AND have a higher purpose or meaning to their life.

Most people when they reach their deathbed want to know 'Has My Life Been Useful?'

Samuel Hahnemann's (the discoverer of Homeopathy) wrote his own words for his eulogy: **'Non inutilis vixi`:** which is Latin for **'I have not lived in vain'**

I will explain in more detail how to make sure your life is lived on purpose, not in vain...

Chapter 3

How to Identify an Indigo using Astrology

When I first heard about Indigos, and being an Astrologer, I thought if what was proposed was true: i.e. that this generation is radically different from previous ones, there must be an Astrological explanation.

As I explained in my article on my website, I investigated by asking people that *knew* they were Indigo, if they would kindly give me their birth data and I recorded and analysed the results. Out of the first 100 people, 95 of them had one-sided charts.

Now, having a one-sided chart isn't rare. Every now and then the planets line up but what is more rare is when the outer planets come together, because they take longer to go through the Zodiac.

I'll explain.

As we already know, there are 12 signs of the Zodiac from Aries to Pisces. These signs are actually mathematical divisions of the sky. They were originally based on the locations of the constellations of stars that were 'behind' them, but today they are calculated by the spring solstice, when the Sun enters the bit of the sky we call Aries.

The Telescope Planets

The two planets that we are going to discuss were 'discovered' way after the original planets, as they can only be seen with a telescope. The Babylonian Astrologers could only see the planets with the naked eye, so these outer planets wouldn't have been visible to them.

There are three outer planets: Uranus, Neptune and Pluto, but the ones that indicate Indigo-ness are the first two. Pluto is involved with the Indigos' parents' generation, so I won't discuss Pluto here. (That's my next book!)

Plus Pluto can never match-up exactly with the orbits of Neptune and Uranus. I've checked from -226BC to the year 2335 and Pluto ends up opposite Uranus and Neptune quite regularly, but never matches exactly. The nearest they got together was in the year -56BC when Uranus and Neptune were in the sign of Cancer and Pluto was one sign away in Gemini.

In our solar system the planets, the bits in the sky that orbit around the Sun, are in this order of distance from the Sun:

The Sun, Mercury, Venus, Earth, the Moon, Mars, Jupiter, Saturn, Uranus, Neptune and Pluto.

However, in Astrology we work using how the planets look from our viewpoint on Earth, so the order goes:

Sun, Moon, Mercury, Venus, Mars, Jupiter, Saturn, Uranus, Neptune, Pluto

(We call all of them planets, while strictly speaking the Sun isn't a planet, it's a star.)

The planets that help us identify an Indigo are Uranus and Neptune.

Uranus

I love Uranus. He's my favourite planet. Funny really considering I'm a Pisces, I ought to have a love for Neptune my ruling planet but I find too much Neptune stops you getting out of bed ...

So Uranus.

The whole discovery of Uranus by a chap called William Herschel, sums up the energy of the planet and its reflected expression through western mankind. It was a sudden discovery and one that was completely unexpected.

I live in Bath in the West Country of the UK where Uranus was discovered. I have been to the Hershel Museum quite a few times. You can buy a little pamphlet about William or look at his Astronomy equipment and other more personal things behind glass in cabinets. To report the story so long after the event hardly does it justice but suffice to say William Herschel was a talented man.

The Scorpio Delves Deep

William was born in Hanover in Germany in 1738, making him a Scorpio (intense) with Moon in Capricorn (emotionally robust) when, interestingly enough, Uranus was in the sign of Capricorn. (And it's the coming together of Uranus and Neptune in Capricorn that marks the centre of the Indigo energies).

William started life as an oboist in the Hanoverian Guards. Having been posted to England with the Guards he was so impressed by life there that he moved to the UK. After a time he moved to Bath and in 1780 set-up shop as a musician. During the day he entertained the locals with recitals of his own compositions. He taught music too, using the cello, oboe and organ and lived with his devoted sister Caroline. (Sun Pisces, Moon Cancer)

But at night he came alive and watched the stars. He was what could only be described politely as 'an amateur'. All the same, he discovered Uranus. There was William an astronomical geek, looking through his telescope at night, tracking the path of one planet in particular. He experimented with telescopic lenses and developed a lens that meant he could see further into space and track the movements of planets no-one would have been capable of before. Without this extra strong lens he never would have seen the planet at all.

Although William was an amateur astronomer, his discoveries and technical achievements had a big impact at the time. His ambition was to extend telescopic vision into space by increasing the size of the actual telescopes. Although being best remembered for the discovery of Uranus, William was also responsible for increasing the dimensions of the Milky Way, discovering the satellites of Saturn and other planets, the rotation of Saturn's rings as well as the motion of binary stars.

During the time he lived at 19 New King Street, Bath, William experimented with techniques for grinding and polishing specula mirrors. In 1789 he completed work on what was then, the world's largest telescope which was a reflector, 40 ft in length with a massive 48 inch mirror which proved very problematic to cast and polish. It was built and used in the gardens of Observatory House, Slough, which is where it stayed until it was destroyed in a gale in 1839. Through his observations of the sun, William accidentally discovered the existence of infra-red radiation. Using thermometers and prisms he conducted experiments which led to a series of papers being published in 1800 on the discovery of the independent behaviour of radiant heat and visible light.

The Astronomer and the King

King George III had a fascination for science, and astronomy in particular. He kept abreast of the latest discoveries and patronised the leading astronomers of the day. When William made his discovery of Uranus on the 13th March 1781, the Sun was in the sign of Pisces (Caroline's sign, it was 3 days before her birthday) and the Moon was in the sign of Scorpio, William's Sun sign.

William's fame quickly spread and the King was duly impressed.

This led to a royal appointment and a grant of £200 a year to further his research at the King's seat, Datchet, near Windsor, and latterly at Slough. In return he was expected to show the Royal Family and their guests interesting astronomical observations. Later the King rewarded Herschel with £4,000 towards the construction of his 40ft telescope as well as a payment of £50 per year for his sister Caroline.

The planet Uranus was first seen in the night sky in 1690 by John Flamsteed, but he thought it was a star. He catalogued it and called it '34 Tauri'.

William understood it was *not* a star and named it the 'Georgian Planet' in honour of his patron, King George III. Others at that time called the planet Herschel after the man who discovered it.

God of The Heavens

As most of the previous planetary discoveries had been named after ancient gods from Greek mythology, the name Uranus came into common use around 1850. Uranus was the god of the heavens. He was the earliest supreme god.

In the Olympian creation myth, Uranus came every single night to cover the earth and mate with Gaia, but he hated the children she bore him and imprisoned Gaia's youngest children in Tartarus[1]; a deep, gloomy place, a pit, or an abyss used as a dungeon of torment and suffering that resides beneath the underworld[2].

To facilitate her revenge for imprisoning her children, Gaia shaped a great flint sickle and asked her sons to castrate Uranus. Only Cronus (Saturn) was willing: he ambushed his father and castrated him, casting that which was severed into the sea. From the blood which spilled from Uranus onto the Earth came forth the Gigantes[3], the three snake-haired avenging Furies. From that which was cast into the sea came forth Aphrodite[4]. After his castration, the Sky came no more to cover the Earth at night, but stayed up above.

Strange Orbit

In Astronomy Uranus takes 84 years to circle the Sun. Its orbit is strange and involves tilting at almost 98 degrees. In Astrology it takes 84 years for Uranus to make a complete circuit of the Zodiac, so you will have to get to the minimum of that age to see your 'Uranus Return'.

The astrological community then had to make a correlation between the activity of Uranus and the western population and it was decided, after much argument and discussion that Uranus would 'rule' the sign Aquarius.

Today the paths of Astrology and Astronomy have diverged. Astronomy went on to become a 'science' and Astrology has become a sort of pagan belief system, maybe nearer to its early roots.

Doesn't bother me. We can have plenty of fun without being a 'science'....

---

1. http://en.wikipedia.org/wiki/Tartarus
2. http://en.wikipedia.org/wiki/Hades
3. http://en.wikipedia.org/wiki/Gigantes
4. http://en.wikipedia.org/wiki/Aphrodite

The keywords we use to describe Uranus are: freedom, individuality, ideas ... and suddenness and being the 'ruler' of Aquarius which I consider to be a fitting choice. *'Uranus timed its entrance with flair, to coincide with three major social revolutions also intent on disrupting the established order of things. The American and French revolutions and the advent of the Industrial Revolution.'*[4]

Neptune

All the signs of the Zodiac, from Aries to Pisces have a 'Planet' that looks after them. We use the term 'rules' them. You could say in a way, that they 'come' from this planet because the planet describes the motivating forces of the sign. The rulerships were decided after years of argument and discussion amongst various astrologers (and is still in dispute each time a new planet is discovered).

Near Miss by Galileo

Neptune was nearly discovered by Galileo who first saw it while he was observing the Jupiter system on 28 December 1612.

After the discovery of Uranus in 1781 by William Hershel in Bath, UK (where I live) astronomers continued to observe the night sky and track the movements of other celestial bodies. However, Neptune's discovery wasn't made by observation. The astronomers who were working on the case used 'mathematical astronomy'. Uranus wasn't moving as predictions said it would, so the astronomers concluded that another planet must be affecting its orbit.

Neptune was recorded several more times, without being recognized as a planet, over the following years.

Lalande a French astronomer, recorded Neptune on the 8th and 10th of May 1795 thinking that it was a star.

William Herschel's son John Herschel, who was involved with the discovery, recorded Neptune on 14 July 1830 also believing it to be a star.

Mathematical Discovery

However, a French chap named Urbain Le Verrier, who worked at the Paris Observatory, used mathematical calculation to prove its existence and he

"discovered a star with the tip of his pen, without any instruments other than the strength of his calculations alone."

The date he discovered it was 23rd September 1846, when Uranus (sudden happenings) and Pluto (deep transformation) were both in the sign of Aries (interestingly Uranus is in Aries while I'm writing this book!)

He received many honors and widespread recognition for his achievement.

The Times carried the headline on the 1st October 1846: "*Le Verrier's planet found*".

George Airy and John Couch Adams were the two other astronomers, who independently worked on 'finding' the planet.

In the aftermath of the discovery, there was much nationalistic rivalry between the French and the British over who had priority for the discovery and eventually, after considerable argument, it was decided to give the credit to both Urbain Le Verrier and Adams together. Their discovery was called Neptune.

So Neptune the planet was 'found' not by observation, as most of the other planets were discovered, but by mathematical means i.e. Urbain Le Verrier sat there, working out the movements of Uranus, which he (and John Couch Adams) deduced must be influenced by the orbit of another planet, because it was not moving as they thought it would.

Margaret E Hone wrote in 1951 in her 'Modern Text Book of Astrology'[10] more than 100 years after Neptune was discovered: '*This planet has to do with what hides itself from view, hence it is the most difficult for which to find a suitable one-word description.*'

She then goes on to use the words

'nebulousness, impressionability, artistic, dreamy, emotional, idealistic, imaginative, sensitive, subtle, sentimental, woolly, wandering and unstable' to convey the sort of themes that Neptune governs.

God of The Sea

Plenty has been written about Neptune in myth. The Romans called him the God of the sea, (the Greeks called him Poseidon) and he was Zeus' younger brother. He carried a trident which had three prongs, as is seen it its glyph that Astrologers now use.

In Roman legend, he was given the sea as his realm and he took over the Greek God Poseidon's job of getting into tempestuous rages. His wife, Amphitrite, gave birth to a son called Triton. He was also famed for having love affairs and was the father to several other children who were wild and cruel. He was worshipped as the god of navigation and temples were erected in his honor. Both the Greeks and later the Romans felt this God controlled the seas and when angry would cause storms and shipwrecks.

170-Year Cycle

The cycle of Uranus and Neptune planets travelling through the Zodiac and becoming conjunct takes 170 years.

The last time it happened was 1821 the next time it will happen will be 2165.

So you can understand this isn't your average planetary happening.

Richard Tarnas, in his 'Cosmos and Psyche' [7] tells us about all the conjunctions, oppositions and squares of these planets, but we only need to consider the conjunction.

This is when the two planets 'come together' = 'conjunct' in the same sign.

As they both travel at different speeds, their coming together is auspicious because it blends their two energies.

Neptune is all about connecting with the divine and Uranus is all about sudden, inspirational happenings.

The Internet, which has developed along with Indigos, didn't really become commercial and in people's homes until the late 1990s when Uranus and Neptune were in the sign of Capricorn.

I wanted to know why or where the idea came from that Indigos were more psychic than their predecessors. I concluded it was because of these two planets, but because they eventually ended-up in the sign of Capricorn, these Indigo's psychic ability is practical not airy-fairy. They just *know* when things will be good or bad.

Uranus' and Neptune's Orbits

Uranus Neptune

1979 Scorpio Sagittarius

1985 Sagittarius Capricorn

1988 Capricorn Capricorn

1995 Aquarius Capricorn

1998 Aquarius Aquarius

2002 Pisces Aquarius

As you will see in the above table, the sign changes of Uranus and Neptune don't totally match up until they both reach the sign Capricorn.

Uranus' orbit is 84 years and Neptune is much longer taking at least 164 years to travel through the Zodiac, so the last time these two planets were together in the sign of Capricorn was 1821. The time before that they were together in the sign of Sagittarius in 1650 and the next time they will become conjunct is the year 2165....which nobody reading this book will witness!

Richard Tarnas also makes the point that these dates aren't significant in themselves, they're just dates when planets come together and they do that all the time. What's interesting is, when they come together strange things happen creatively. There are no extra amounts of wars, or famines or catastrophes, but the gestalt of the planet's psyche is expressed through the minds of the more creative members of the time.

Creative People

If we look at what artist's and musician's create during these conjunctions, we can tell far more about the planet's influence, because a creative person sometimes expresses something from their 'higher self' rather than just to make a profit.

During 1650 most artists painted pictures of religious people, as Sagittarius is the sign concerned with 'faith'

The artists born during 1821 painted in a down-to-earth (Capricorn) way, beautiful sceneries, and practical depictions of events. Ford Maddox Brown's most famous painting 'Work' is of some workers building a new sewer....

The next total conjunction was in the year 1998 and lasted until 2002. If you were born during this conjunction, your genius will involve freedom of mind, anything to do with computers and the unity of humankind.

Now, if you are a Sun sign that is near to the winter months, your chart shape is going to be very clustered. Say, for instance, you're a Capricorn born in 1988, you will have your Sun, Mercury, Uranus and Neptune in Capricorn.

Clustered Charts

I talk a lot about clustered charts. It must be my most used astrological expression! I suppose I'm a bit obsessed by it as I find it extraordinary that so many people between the years of 1979 and 2002 were born with this chart shape.

When we talk about a chart shape what we mean is the positioning in the circle of the horoscope that the planets make in the chart.

A guy called Marc Edmund Jones[8] wrote about chart shapes in the late 1800s and I agree when he says making an overall assessment of the charts *before* you start is a jolly good idea.

There are lots of chart shapes. They're called a Bucket, Seesaw, Splash, Bowl or Splay.

My chart is called a Splash as all my planets are dotted unevenly around the circle.

In reality the chart shape is formed by the planets being in certain parts of the sky on the day of birth.

Of all the charts that I have looked at and analysed, which now runs into the thousands, it always surprises me is how so many of them have the Moon as part of the cluster.

Let's go back a bit

The Moon changes sign every two days.

The Sun changes sign every 30 days or so.

So many of the people that have contacted me about the Indigo phenomenon have their Moon in the same signs as the other planets. Rarely do I find a chart where the Moon is opposite (which it could very easily be) the signs in the cluster.

Anyway the point I'm making is from 1979 to 2002 as two outer planets travelled through the signs from Scorpio to Pisces means that anyone who is the Sun sign Scorpio, Sagittarius, Capricorn, Aquarius, or Pisces will have their outer planets in those same signs, making their chart more bunched up and clustered.

If you are a Taurus, Gemini or Cancer your Sun sign will be opposite Uranus and Neptune's conjunction. Your chart is more likely to look like a seesaw, with 5 planets on one side and 5 on the other.

This is quite a nice shape and gives you an ability to stand back from the deep, intensity that Indigos can have and gives you some objectivity.

Chapter 4

OK, I'm an Indigo! Now what?

This is a very good question!

And one that is asked quite a bit.

So, you've found out that your planets are all on one side of the circle, you were born during the Neptune/Uranus conjunction, you have a burning desire to live your life your way...but your life seems one long, hard struggle.

I sympathise.

I hated almost every minute of my teens and early 20's. There was stress galore, work seemed to engulf all my time. Nothing I attempted seemed to work out. I was a frazzled wreck. I don't know how you personally feel but I expect you're asking lots of questions and not getting too much in the way of answers.

The Indigo phenomenon has had a big build-up and quite understandably people expect something to 'happen' the minute they become 'enlightened'.

This is just a random sample of things that people ask me:

"Hello, I believe I am an indigo child, now what?"

A jolly good question!

"Dear Mary, I identified with almost all of the items on the indigo child checklist. I have always had feelings of clairvoyance, intuitiveness, and a natural knowing of one's future. This issue is I'm a jack-of-all-trades and it's bitter sweet. I am intrigued and successful in a lot of affairs. I now want to be famous for leaving a mark on our Planet before I go. I live by Mother Teresa's: "Spread love everywhere you go. Let no one ever come to you without leaving happier." I also read people and am usually accurate. I seek out your guidance, thank you :) peace and love M"

This book was written to help answer all those questions, in plain English and to offer a little guidance on the road to wherever you are going.

Knowing you are Indigo isn't an answer though and can bring even more questions.

"I'm M. I'm 35 yrs old. I'm from Northern Ireland. I've only by accident come across something on indigo. Never heard of it before and it was like having an illness and finally getting a diagnosis."

OK, so you've got the 'diagnosis', now what?

Aren't bells supposed to ring?

Or people to greet you in the street and lay flowers at your feet?

Aren't others supposed to give you some slack and recognize your Indigo-ness dammit!!!

Unfortunately, that is not going to happen.

Knowing you are Indigo is the Beginning, not the End.

If we listen to other Indigos who have already made the journey, we can learn a lot.

Vadim Zeland is a Russian author of the mind-body-spirit series of books called Reality Transurfing.

I have read all of his books.

I know his is an Indigo as we have communicated by email but I am sworn to secrecy.

I know he has the answers and the solutions that the Indigo generation needs. Except his 'message' was written in Russian and when it got translated into English, as lot of his solutions didn't come through strongly enough to make them mainstream. You might never have heard of him, which is a pity, as his words are inspirational and he's a contemporary of yours. So he's got lots of solutions! His series of books has sold over 1,200,000 copies in Russia alone and have been translated into over 18 different languages.

He talks about 'The Pendulums': the large organisations that exist like the government or religions or (in the UK) the NHS health sector, or the Tax Office or the Armed Forces, postal services, or even MacDonald's. Big companies that are there to make a profit, or keep people dancing to a certain tune. Because they are so big, they have a life of their own and he talks about how all they do is suck your energy, or use your skills or resources, so they can continue to stay 'alive.'

I've worked for large organisations and they have to train their staff to think in a certain way. Crickey! How scary is that? Having your thinking process influenced by your employer.... all under the banner of 'Because You are Worth It' or 'I'm loving it'. These aren't real attributes, they're part of a brain washing exercise to keep employees churning out the work that's needed to keep the company (pendulum) going.

Now, none of this matters if you're quite happy working to someone else's mantra. If you're just doing it 'for the money' or to 'pay the rent' that's fine enough, provided underneath you still do the things you love, or at the very least are true to your inner self.

Vadim describes how you can do this without getting sucked into the corporate entanglements that will leave your soul flat. More details on his website http://zelands.com/

Most of the emails I get are from people wanting to find their life purpose. Having a life purpose was hardly a consideration in my younger years and not one I worried about when I was a teen, but now it's a constant quest for the Indigos. The Internet is helpful but also a curse as far as this goes, in that we can discover plenty of things we didn't know but does that new knowledge enhance our lives?

I think not.

We need to remember that a person's life purpose can't be determined by a few searches on the Internet.

You can't Google" 'Why was I created?' and expect a sensible answer. You'll get plenty of results, but they'll all be religious.

But that's what people DO want to know, when they have a quiet moment, or their life is a struggle, or things aren't panning out as they'd like.

Why am I here?

What does it all mean?

Where am I going?

These sorts of questions can burn through your brain and cause headaches late at night after sleepless hours.

We all want to know the answer to 'why am I here?'

If you've ever had a near death experience, you'll stop asking that question but you don't have to risk death to find the answer!

What you do have to do is formulate the question correctly.

Finding a Life Purpose

Now, I'd just like to make a distinction between a life purpose and a job. A job is what you do to pay the rent, have food to eat, be able to buy things, go out with friends and have a hobby or interest.

A life purpose is what's underneath your job. It's your reason for existing. This causes an enormous amount of confusion.

I hear people complain that they weren't created to work in a dead-end job and pack shelves in a supermarket, or serve customers, or work in a call centre or a factory.

OK, so you're not going to do these jobs? So how will you earn a living? How will you pay the rent? If you're in the UK, are you expecting the government to carry on paying you money to sit at home, *thinking* about getting a job?

Let's get some definitions going, and then we can answer these questions a little more clearly.

A purpose is:

Object to be attained, thing intended, intention to act, resolution, determination.

A life is:

State of existence as a living individual, living person.

So a Life Purpose is a State of Living with Intention (to act)

This makes a life purpose something that's in the future. Somewhere that you won't get to just yet. Something that you're working towards but might not know how to get there.

Doesn't sound helpful, does it?

Now, what if you had everything in your life that you needed now?

What if you had enough money, and a purpose and everything was sorted?

How would you feel then?

Let's see what happens if we just make that definition a bit more robust and make it:

A Life Purpose is a State of Living with Intent.

And what is intent? Attentively occupied.

So, let's formulate that again:

A Life Purpose is a State of Being Attentively Occupied

In other words, if you're thinking about what you are doing, while you are doing it, then your life purpose is in the here and now.

So, there you are putting today's mail on your desk in a busy office, sorting through to find the envelopes to give to your boss. Or you're in the store-room, looking for some size 16 black leggings to go on a rail in the ladies-wear section, or you're answering the phone to someone who is *really* cross that what they ordered hasn't arrived...

And in each of these scenarios, you could be thinking of a million-and-one things *other* than what you are actively engaged in doing...and that's NOT living a life with intent. That's being somewhere other than where you are now.

We could make it clearer by asking about what's the opposite of a life purpose?

It could be a life where it seems as if nothing is meaningful and everyday is a struggle. Where you see your friends as more successful as you. Where all the studying you might have done at university hasn't automatically brought you a job, let alone a career path.

Notice what you are doing when you think like this.

You're living in the future again, where everything would be lovely 'only if' you had this and 'if only you had that'.

Be In The Here and Now

What if you actually lived in the here and now? If you accepted exactly what your present life circumstances are, even if they're really bad and you are sleeping rough. Once you accept where you are, then you can work towards where you'd *prefer* to be.

Eckhart Tolle describes this is much more detail in his wonderful book 'The Power of Now':

'Wherever You Are, Be There Totally.

See if you can catch yourself complaining, in either speech or thought, about a situation you find yourself in..... To complain is always non-acceptance of what *is.* It invariably carries an unconscious negative charge. When you complain, you make yourself into a victim. When you speak out, you are in your power. So change the situation by taking action....leave the situation or accept it. All else is madness.'

So if you don't want to be in the boring, dull job you are in, accept that it is a means-to-an-end. If you're not in a job at all, get out there and find one.

You can get some help by reading *Getting the Job You Want: A Practical Guide* By Denise Taylor

Your life purpose is right here, right now, not waiting for you in the future.

But, I can hear you saying, surely my life purpose can't be working in a fast food restaurant?

Why not?

If you didn't work there, people wouldn't eat the food, suppliers would be out of work, all the links in the chain would break AND you'd be out of work.

Surely it's better for you to work there until you find something else suitable, or you might work there long enough to get a promotion, or earn enough money to move somewhere else where you can earn more?

Your Life Purpose isn't What you Do, but the Way that you do it

Let me make the distinction again. Your life purpose isn't what you do, but the way that you do it.

Say you were working for a really worthwhile organisation, something like Greenpeace. And you worked everyday in an angry frame of mind, and you barked at people when they spoke to you and you got into arguments in meetings, and you were always late and back-stabbed all your peers, it wouldn't matter to your soul one jot that you job title was 'Senior Peace Conciliator' if you weren't in your 'self', peaceful at all.

When you go through life observing people, you'll sometimes find people that might be in really humble jobs, and they've got a happy family at home, and children and a loving wife. They emit peace everywhere they go. That's a life purpose. When you live your life, whatever it is, with meaning.

The Carers Who Cared

When my youngest sister who has Down's syndrome came to live near me, so I could organise her care as my mother had got Alzheimer's, we had a team of carers who looked after her 24/7. They slept over, washed and dressed her, read her stories, cooked her food and took her out to her job in a charity shop. My 'job' was to oversee their employment and check my sister was happy and well cared for.

Some of her early carers seemed face-to-face to be loving, caring people but when my back was turned they were on their phones, chatting with their friends, ignoring my sister and her needs.

Some wouldn't even sit in the same room as her. I soon learned who were the best to employ and eventually we had a lovely team of wonderful ladies who worked round-the-clock to care for her.

One was a brilliant cook and would help my sister makes tasty meals.

One loved the outdoors and nature and would take her for short walks to see the local horses and birds (my sister is a keen bird watcher)

One knew how to weave and would help my sister with her weaving and think of creative ways to help her to still do the hobbies she enjoyed.

One was very good at helping her feel safe and cared for and knew all the things she liked to hear like family names and little jokes. This lady had no degrees, no qualifications, was a mother and a wife near retirement, but her manner was kind and she was living a life well.

Each of them had a certain way of helping. Now none of these ladies could say that their work was saving the planet, or changing the world....but in my mind they were saving just one person's life and that was as valuable as any work you can have and I to this day deeply appreciate their loving care.

So your life purpose isn't in the future, it isn't a job or a badge you wear or a title you have or the training you've got or the exams you sit, it's the way you live your life from start to finish.

Being Kind and Caring

If you're kind and caring and helpful as you can be, you're already living your life purpose.

If you think of others and consider if what you're doing will help or hinder, that's a life lived with purpose.

So your work is different from your life purpose.

In my lifetime I've worked in an old-fashioned ladies underwear shop, the Post-Office, first as a delivery person and then later as a counter clerk, selling encyclopedias door-to-door, in a large branch of MacDonald's putting cheese on burgers (it was only for a day but I learned a lot about fast food!), as a chambermaid in a large hotel, in various retail outlets, in a petrol station selling fuel and oil, in small shops and big stores, as a volunteer in a charity shop, as a waitress in an Italian Restaurant, (I really enjoyed that job as it was a family run business, and I got fed!) as a receptionist for a company that sold adult leisure toys including yo-yos and skateboards, in a local call centre for a mobile phone company.....quite a few varied 'jobs', some more interesting than others.

For a short time, in my teens I read palms and cards but as I had no idea how to 'be' self-employed. If I'd had some training in running my own business I might have persisted but I had no idea how to register as self-employed or pay my tax or national insurance. Eventually I got a job in a local chemist shop so I could pay my rent.

I worked my way up from being a retail assistant to eventually branch manager in various retailers before I took the big career change to where I am today by training to be a Homeopath. I'm a self-taught Astrologer and I'd still got all the experience I'd gained from those early readings, which I carried on in my spare time. All those years of varied jobs have added to my life experience and cannot be considered a waste of time.

The Indigo MacDonald's Manager

A few years ago I met a lovely young man who was an archetypical indigo. He had the most clustered chart I have ever seen and he was the manager of a branch of McDonald's. He had a lovely gentle manner and a soft voice and genuinely cared about the staff that worked for him.

He had a degree and plenty of brains and he knew he wouldn't be working there forever because he had a vision. He knew that his work was paying the bills and keeping him busy. He didn't actually mind that job, the only thing he objected to was being the key holder and getting called out late at night if the alarms went off.

His vision was to work in the field of his degree, which was in marine biology, and he had made himself a five-year plan to get there. He came for a reading with me just to check that he was on the right track, which he was and we discussed his next steps.

The one major difference with indigo phenomena is there is no one central control centre. There is no one organisation that runs it. There aren't really any legitimate indigo organisations that can help you, unlike say the Samaritans.

And anyway having an Indigo organisation is counterintuitive, as indigos don't like to be controlled or to be directed in anyway.

Remember Vadim's advice, to stay away from Pendulums, as they drain your energy.

If you had an Indigo Organisation it would soon turn into a Pendulum and would start swinging in ways to take your energy. It, the organisation, wouldn't care about you, it would only care about itself, so what would be the use in joining?

Being Self-Employed

When it comes to work, which we all have to do unless we're royalty (!) I'm surprised that more Indigos aren't becoming self-employed.

With Uranus the planet of freedom and Neptune the planet of sixth sense, it makes more sense for them to be their own employer. It's a pity that schools don't give lessons on self-employment and there is too much emphasis on "further education", which is all very fine if there is a job at the end of it. But if you have a degree in a certain subject surely it would make sense to work in the field for yourself?

You can register as self-employed at the website http://www.hmrc.gov.uk/selfemployed/register-selfemp.htm

You will also need to register for Class 2 and Class 4 National Insurance. Class 2 contributes towards certain benefits and your state pension and Class 4 is basically a tax on your earnings that you have to pay if you earn more than a certain amount of money at the moment it's around £9,000 but that will change every year.

What a lot of people don't realise is, the money you earn from self-employment, (or sole trader/sole proprietorship) is all yours, providing you don't earn *more* than the tax threshold. If you do earn more, than you're only taxed on that amount.

In the USA self-employment is slightly different and is called sole proprietorship. People like freelance writers and work that involves just your own skills like being a therapist, life-coach, making crafts, being a photographer, dog-walker, tarot reader or psychic, would come under this title. You are responsible for paying your taxes (and Medicare) which are the lowest rates for the different types of small businesses.

More details here

http://www.sba.gov/content/sole-proprietorship-0

http://www.irs.gov/Businesses/Small-Businesses-&-Self-Employed

How Palmistry Can Help

Not everyone is suited to self-employment. It is much easier now (in the UK, I can't speak for other countries).

Palmistry can help you find out if you're suited to it.

As you will know, all your fingers have fingerprints.

There are 3 basic types: Whorl, Loop and Arch.

This is what they look like:

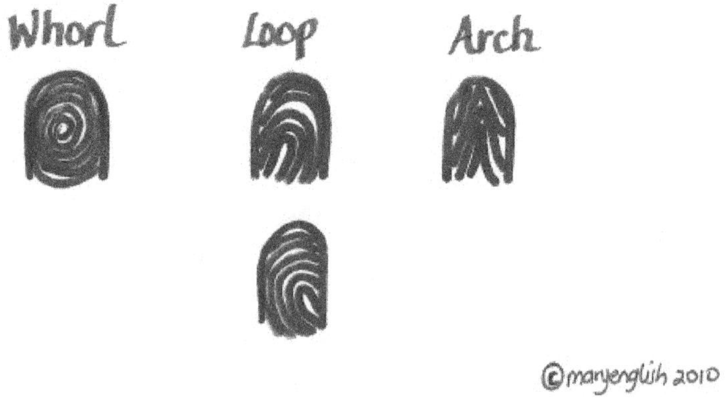

Whorl

Looks like a whirlpool, with the finger-print pattern going round and round itself.

Loop

Looks like a whorl but it ends on the side of the finger, on the left or right and doesn't go round and round in a circle, but in a loop.

Arch

Looks like a hill or a mound, with the pattern pointing upwards. Some arches are higher than others.

In Palmistry, the pointy finger/first finger represents how you get along in the world, where you're going, as, if you think about it, it's the finger you use to point. We use this as an indicator of the sort of work you're suited to. Your right hand (if you're right handed) represents your future or your conscious self and your left hand represents your past or your unconscious self. (Reverse if left-handed)

Have a look at the print pattern on these fingers.

Not everyone has the same prints on both hands. I don't. I have a Whorl on my left hand and a Loop on my right hand.

To be happily self-employed you need at least one Whorl on your pointy fingers.

Whorls denote someone who is creative, likes doing things themselves, doesn't like taking orders.

Loops indicate being OK with change, being adaptable, being able to 'fit-in' and preferring someone else to take the flak.

Arches represent someone who works best with a forward plan. Depending on how high the Arch is, depends on how far into the future you need to plan.

Now, if you want to be *completely* self-employed, (as in not needing money from anyone or anywhere else) it would help to have Whorls on both hands.

If you've only got them on one hand, you might need a partner or husband to support you as well, or benefits for working parents, or a tax break, assistance from a charity of some kind or you could barter your services and do exchanges....

If you've got Loops, you will feel better having a boss and a job and someone else to make the decisions and I don't really recommend it unless you get lots of support. You might be best suited to part self-employment, part employment.

If you have Arches, you can be self-employed but you must make yourself a forward plan and write down how much you need to earn to live, and stick to it. You might be self-employed for a while until you find work that suits.

You Don't Have to Save the World Just Yet

Now that you have found out you are an Indigo, there are a few things that will help you settle into the idea a little better.

1. You don't have to save the world, the planet and the dolphins or 'convert' anyone else to your own way of thinking.

2. You can live your own life, how you'd like it to be, without worrying that you're wasting your time, or not fulfilling your purpose

3. If you're sensitive to people and things, spend less time with what makes you feel bad. If you've got lots of electrical items in your room, get an extension lead and turn everything off at night....*including* your mobile phone. Or at least leave your phone in another room. If you're very sensitive to other's suffering, don't watch the news or hang around with people that make you feel bad.

4. Give-up, reduce, stay away from recreational drugs, cigarettes, too much alcohol, high caffeine or high sugar drinks. These are all chemicals and will affect your thinking and your long-term health

5. Write a list of how you'd like your life to be in 5 years time, then make one small step today to nearing that goal.

6. Enjoy your hobbies and pleasures but don't let them overtake your life. Be as balanced as you can.

Chapter 5

What is Belief? How does Astrology Help?

I think I can safely say that the indigo concept is a spiritual one. The evolution that Jan and Lee are talking about isn't physical. It's spiritual but most Indigos don't want to follow a religion or go to church.

But what happens if you wanted to explore your spiritual self without touching into religion?

What happens then?

My trusty dictionary defines 'Believe' as: accept as true or as conveying truth (*I believe it, him, what you say, that it is so)* think, suppose, have (esp. religious faith) have faith in the existence of, have confidence in.

In chapter 3 we discussed the two outer planets: Uranus and Neptune. They are generational planets and take a long time to travel through each sign of the Zodiac. The only outer planet that will return to the same placement as in your birth chart is Uranus, provided you live to be at least 84 years old.

The planet that Astrologers use to help them understand someone's beliefs is called Jupiter.

King of the Planets

Unlike Uranus, Neptune and Pluto, Jupiter was never 'discovered' as even the Babylonians, the original instigators of astrology, could see it with the naked eye from Earth.

Astronomers call Jupiter "the undisputed king of the planets" as it is the first of the so-called gas giants.

It is so big and one of the brightest objects in the heavens. Jupiter twinkles by reflecting light from the Sun, however it emits more than twice as much energy as it receives from the sun and is one of the noisiest objects in the sky.

It also has a powerful magnetic field.

It's amazing to think that even though Jupiter is between 893 million and 964 million kilometres from the Earth, I can still see it in my back garden.

Now keeping in mind that the Earth itself is (at the equator) 12,756 kilometres wide, (diameter) then Jupiter is over 70,006 times the width of the Earth away from us, and I can still see it. So imagine then, that it must be pretty big!

Gas Giant

Jupiter is made of hydrogen and helium gas with some methane mixed in, so there is no solid surface to walk on like that of the Moon. These gases form beautiful horizontal stripes across its surface. It travels so fast it makes a complete rotation every ten hours so it makes you wonder if you'd grow older quicker living there!

Spinning around it are sixty-three satellites, four of which are called Moons and they can be seen through binoculars, and look like a little string of pearls.

Now, Astrology takes the description of a planet, mixes it with some key-words and 'bingo' produces its attributes.

So.

As Jupiter is a gas-giant, we talk in Astrology about it magnifying and making things that it connects with it bigger.

Someone with Jupiter in their chart, near their Sun sign, will be one of those people given to 'overdoing' things or exaggerating.

We also use some of the stories from myths and legends (this is the bit I like) and add it to the mix. In the Greek myths Jupiter was called Zeus and Eve Jackson in: 'Jupiter An Astrologer's Guide' describes him like this:

"Zeus is generally depicted as a man of middle years, bearded and imposing, wearing his aegis or goatskin of divine power and his cloak sometimes sky blue, sometimes the deep blue of the night sky, spangled with stars. Among his many titles are King, Saviour, Father, Descender,

Kindly One, Friend, Giver of Completeness, God of Marriage, Protector of Strangers, Counsellor, Cloud-Gatherer, Thunderer, Protector of Oaths."9

So here we have 'someone' who is a fatherly figure, friendly, kind and philosophical...but also, when he's had a bad day, capeable of throwing his thunderbolts and scaring the natives.

When the Babylonians originally viewed Jupiter, they called him Marduk: the son of the Sun God. In the myths of the time, he organised the chaos of the universe, created the constellations, decided the boundary lines of the fixed year and also:

" *Set up three stars for each of the 12 months*"

Quite a busy chap!

As Astrology travelled across the world from east to west via Greece, and developed and changed as it went, Jupiter became what he is today, the Great Benefactor. There to guide us and help us on our life journey, our spiritual path.

If you're struggling with your spirituality, it will help you to study a bit about your Jupiter, it's sign and placement. It will help you learn about the *sort* of spirituality that you will feel more comfortable with.

Here are the general meanings of Jupiter in each sign of the Zodiac:

As Jupiter takes approximately 12 years to travel through the Zodiac, most of the people in your class at school, will have their Jupiter in the same sign, or the one either side.

This is why following a certain religion or faith is OK if your teacher or parents have the same Jupiter sign as you.

If they don't, then you'll never agree on what belief is....

Aries

Jupiter in Aries will mean you prefer a faith or belief that's fast, active and full of life. You won't want to follow other's dogma, you want to be a leader in your beliefs, not a follower.

Vadim Zeland (author) Starhawk

Taurus

As Taurus is the sign of the material world, physical sensuality and the body your spiritual path might include expression through your body. Maybe Tai Chi, Yoga or Karate. You will more likely enjoy a form of spirituality that is gentle, artistic and beautiful.

Thomas Moore (spiritual writer)

Gemini

Changeable. That's something you will find with your beliefs. They will change with the wind. One day you follow one path, tomorrow the next. As long as you can have some v*ariety* in way your beliefs lie, you will feel happier. You will also enjoy a spiritual path that involves discussion and debate. You might enjoy talking about your beliefs more than living through them.

Oprah Winfrey

Cancer

Your home, family and your roots are your faith. And Cancer is a maternal sign concerned with mothering and tenderness and being able to nurture emotions and feelings. your ancestors and your children will be way your belief lies. You might want to carry on a family tradition, or follow an ancient path.

Byron Katie, Nelson Mandela

Leo

Your spirituality will be bright, sunny and friendly. Not for you long amounts of time in silent contemplation on a mountaintop. You want to be with others, maybe even leading them so they can dance to your tune. You won't be adverse to lavish displays of affection or recognition so you will be suited to means that are demonstrative. You love to celebrate, to party and to enjoy life's goodness.

Masaru Emoto, Alice Walker

Virgo

As Virgo is the sign of specifics and health, you yearn for a form of spirituality that will be clear and defined and good for you and the planet. It will take up a lot of your thinking and could be expressed in writing or communication. You might enjoy reading spiritual texts, or studying religions. You will prefer something clearly defined with as much detail as possible.

Brian Weiss

Libra

Relationships are the key to the sign of Libra. You might express your beliefs better when you're in a partnership than if you were on your own. You will feel more connected to your spiritual purpose when you're in a relationship, as that relationship will bring you closer to your true purpose, which is to be truly loving. If you're very evolved, you might manage that on your own.

Stuart Wilde, Doreen Virtue

Scorpio

Your spirituality will be deep and meaningful, maybe even with a secret edge that you don't discuss with others. There will be issues of trust and loyalty and you won't want to have other people's beliefs imposed on you. You will certainly want something that feels deep and intense.

Dalai Lama, Julian of Norwich, Paulo Coelho

Sagittarius

With Jupiter in it's natural 'home', you are more likely to have strong beliefs that you will stick through thick and thin. Religion might or might not be part of your life, but whatever path you choose it will need to be something that inspires you and makes you feel alive.

Eckhart Tolle, Julia Cameron

Capricorn

If your Jupiter is in Capricorn, you will prefer a more serious faith to follow, maybe something 'old fashioned' or ancient. Something from the past. Modern ideas will seem less appealing. Investigate paganism, Wicca, Gnosticism

Alam lives in Indonesia and has this to say about the Capricorn energy:

Capricorns deal with limitations, structures and strictures. So I think Capricornian expression of faith would include The 10 Commandments, the issue of *halal* (religiously acceptable, such as the flesh of animals being killed swiftly, drained of blood and in the name of Allah; limitations on what foods we can and cannot eat; acceptable types of work etc.) and *haram* (religiously unacceptable, such as food brought with money from thievery, usury, gambling or cheating; the prohibition of liquor etc.), fasting, and prohibitions to pray when one is 'unclean' (in the monthly course or have not cleaned oneself ritually after lovemaking).

Other than limitations, Capricorn is about protection and responsibility. I must still learn about the regulations in other religions and faiths, but in Islam, there is this obligation to give away part of one's wealth to the poor as soon as one's wealth exceeds a certain limit or when there's something left after feeding and clothing and caring for one's family, because all Muslims are brothers and one takes care of one's family. There are the obligations of husbands and wives and parents and children to take care of each other, and there is also special injunction about caring for orphans and the elderly.

The Chinese and Muslim veneration of parents and elders is also a Capricornian thing

Ken Wilber, Edgar Cayce, Linda Goodman

Aquarius

You will prefer your faith to be something modern, or quirky, something that isn't shared by too many people, that gives you the freedom to be 'yourself'. It's important you don't feel dictated to. You will prefer a faith that is people based and compassionate.

Alam tells us:

Aquarius is about rebellion, about being alone in the middle of the crowd, about being special and set aside from one's community, about being *different*, about showing others alternative visions of Heaven and Hell. Aquarius is about lightning flashes and inspirations.

For example, in the Dakota Indian tribes of America, a person who dreams of thunder and lightning means that s/he is chosen to be a *heyoka* or Sacred Clown. S/he must do everything backwards and in reverse in order to enforce what *is* in his/her community.

Something else that comes to mind is the fact that priests and priestesses from all religions tend to clothe themselves in an odd, fantastic - or at least eccentric - manner. Veils, hijabs, surplices, headdresses, robes, mitres, headscarves, hats...you know what I mean.

Being an Air sign, Aquarius also pays attention to specific measurements and calculations, ciphers, numerology etc. (overlapping with Virgo's exactitude). Puzzles, patterns, such as the number of verses in a holy book, the number of beads in all types of rosaries (Hindu, Catholic, Islam) all follow specific patterns.

Richard Tarnas, Thich Nhat Hanh, Louise Hay

Pisces

As Jupiter was the previous ruler to Pisces (it is now Sagittarius) your spirituality is unlikely to be an issue. You know what you believe but maybe you can't quite explain it. It might be inexplicable, unexplainable in words or too mystical to describe easily. It certainly will be somewhere where you hope to touch into all that there is. You might find that poetry or writing or some creative Art will help you touch that spot.

My friend Alam has this to say about Pisces:

Pisces is about change, about illusions and dreams and alternative paths. In this they overlap with Aquarius, because priest(ess) clothing, preparing altars and sacred circles etc. is used as a gateway to another world, another reality.

I think that drug and drink uses in various religious rituals everywhere to transform reality is a Piscean thing. Peyote; bhang; yaje; absinthe; datura; in vino veritas; eat, for this is my flesh, drink, for this is my blood - don't these remind you of the Piscean alternative vision and illusion...?

A ritual I've read in a manga: on the night of the full moon, you pour wine or water into a glass, wait for it to still, and then capture the reflection of the moon in it. When you feel that the moon's essence is imbued in the water or wine, you drink the water and ingest the moon, purifying your heart and soul from all dross matter.

Leonardo da Vinci, Abraham Lincoln, Friedrich Nietzsche, JRR Tolkien

OK, now you have found out what sign your Jupiter is in, and if you also find out where it's located in your chart, you'll have a better understanding of how you can feel more spiritually in-tune with what suits **you.**

One thing that confuses more people than it helps, is the idea that there is only one kind of spirituality.

My early life was blighted by going to a Catholic school run by nuns. I couldn't think of a more unspiritual place because the nuns that ran the place were so out-of-touch with the 'real' world that I lived in.

Religion, Agnostism & Paganism

When I got to my teens, having to attend such a restrictive school irked me considerably and I began to rebel. Luckily (for me) my parents moved to Switzerland and I was sent to an American school. Talk about opposites! This place had a smoking area, for the students! I was in heaven. But because I didn't have long hair, or a cute figure (I looked terrible in jeans), I started to feel out of place again and wished to return to London and the UK. I started to have romantic ideas about

London's streets and parks and all I could think about was what I thought I was missing.

When I look back I realise I had a very good education. One that constantly allowed me to see both sides of life. From 'religious' to 'agnostic' and back again.

I'm now a Pagan, but not because I want to follow anyone or anything but because, finally, I feel at peace, with myself. It was a long time coming...and Astrology helped me do that.

Once you have found out your Jupiter sign and placement, you can do things to 'satisfy' that part of your chart.

In my Surviving the Zodiac series, I explain how getting in touch with your Moon sign helps you feel better, and I suggest practical steps you can make to do that.

So here are the practical steps you can take, for your spiritual self. And I hasten to add in big capitals that this must NOT BE AT THE EXPENSE OF YOUR PRACTICAL SELF .

I've met far too many people that have devoted themselves to what they believe is their soul's purpose, and meanwhile they're borrowing money from their friends and family. Or worse, stealing from them because they believe the world owes them. The world doesn't owe you anything. You're lucky to be here, and alive and having the ability to make choices about your own life now.

I will divide my advice up into the Elements of Earth, Air, Fire and Water.

The Earth signs are Taurus, Virgo and Capricorn

The Air signs are Gemini, Libra and Aquarius

The Fire signs are Aries, Leo and Sagittarius

The Water signs are Cancer, Scorpio and Pisces

If your Jupiter is in an Earth sign, use crystals and earth based products in your rituals. You can also use Yoga or other physical expressions to ground you.

If your Jupiter is in an Air sign, use conversation, written communication, tweets, updates, blogs, poetry and discussion to inspire you. Go outside in the fresh air and meditate to calm your mind if you go into overdrive!

If your Jupiter is in a Fire sign, then use candles, incense, Fire-Walking, bonfires, anything to do with Fire and Heat to help you connect with your deity.

If your Jupiter is in a Water sign, then think of emotional water-based connections like Auro-Soma, Water Shiatsu (now called Watsu), Flower Essences, swimming and being by the sea. Anything that connects you with the divine in a watery way.

Chapter 6

When things go Wrong

As I have worked (and still work) in private practice, helping clients whose lives have got into a tangle, I can safely say I have come across a wide range of issues.

My job is to offer solutions.

Some of them, most of them in fact, are practical, do-able, cheap and easy to put into practice.

I also don't expect my clients to attempt anything I haven't used myself.

Because of the nature of the Internet, and how people can quickly bash off an email asking for help, without really working out what they need the help with, I tend to not respond personally to rushed queries.

This book has been written to help those people that know they truly have a problem they would rather solve themselves.

It goes without saying that if you are suicidal, homeless, or on any sort of long-term drug use or in a violent relationship, then you will need far more help than this book.

These are not issues that self-help can fix.

You need professional guidance, support of peers, a regular treatment programme and lots of time.

However, if you are recently single, finding it hard to hold down a job, feeling dissatisfied with your life in general and harbouring feelings that you'd rather do without, then I can offer some hope and solutions.

As I am also qualified in Homeopathy, I will be suggesting Homeopathic remedies, Bach Flower Essences and other more spiritual remedies.

I will assume by now, that you have made your own birth chart using the website I suggested, as this is the only one I can guarantee will have correct data. Not every website offering free birth charts, or natal charts will have the correct planetary data and might give you a wrong Moon sign or Ascendant.

Asto.com will give you the most accurate information.

Here are examples of the sorts of things I am asked. Some are more shocking than others. Some I respond to immediately, some I wait until I have time. I must stress again, please don't email me if you feel really bad, as there is nothing I can 'do' other than light you a candle. I also find the more extreme email senders don't actually want a consultation or to spend money. Due to the volume of emails I receive, this book was written with that in mind as Indigos prefer to 'find their own way'.

"I am unsure as to how to phrase my request so forgive me, nevertheless. I am in the midst of an indigo driven self-awareness and feel sad, confused, frightened simultaneously. So very unpleasant. Please help if you may. Thank you."

Lack of Sleep

This is the most typical email I receive. It generally is written late at night, after a challenging day for the person. Lack of sleep can make all sorts of worries surface so a priority will always be, get some good rest and work out if it still feels so bad in the morning. Discovering you are Indigo shouldn't bring any negative elements and I tend to think it's because the person may have been surrounded by negative people/ energies and having a good aura cleanse is a good idea.

You can do this easily by getting some white sage. Light one leaf or stick carefully and blow out the flame so the sage is smoldering. It will produce a trail of smoke. It's this smoke you need to waft around your body, taking care you don't breathe too much of it in. Keep wafting it around your body for about 3-4 minutes until you feel a little more settled.

Extinguish the sage carefully.

Go about your business.

Obsessing with Death

This next email was very upsetting for me to receive. I can't (obviously) say that to the person who sent it, but it happens every now and then. Being obsessed with your own death is serious stuff, not to be ignored and needs professional help.

In 2009 I was one semester shy of a biochemistry degree when it dawned on me that the apocalypse was about to happen and that there would be worldwide anarchy very soon. I became paralyzed with fear, sold everything I owned and moved to New Zealand for about a year because I thought it would be a more comfortable place to die. When I ran out of money and realized the apocalypse may not come as soon as I had thought I came back to Boston with no money, no degree and nothing to show for myself but shame. Now I'm in debt to the government almost $60,000 and I have no money, no job, no support structure. I live with my wife whom I married shortly before all of this bless her heart. She works for a catering company and we live quite frugally off of her tiny paycheck. I've always hated living in this world, resenting every dysfunctional system and not caring about money at all. To me the "truth", the answer to the question "why" is the only thing that matters in this world. It is infinitely more important to me than money and jobs and it's really the only thing I think or care about. Now I have a pistol that I plan to use on myself when doomsday happens and I basically just sit here despising myself and wishing the apocalypse would finally happen so I can die without having to hurt those who love me. I see no way out and still feel paralyzed with the same fears as before. My beloved family believes I should be in an asylum and they refuse to indulge any more of my rantings. I see no other way to resolve my worldly problems other than through death. Each detail of the indigo description applies to me in an extreme way and then some. I had never even heard the term until a few days ago. I would love to inform my family of this but don't know how because they're not receptive to anything I say. I'm completely stuck and stagnant. Thank you so much for reading.

I sent this gentleman to a relevant website in his area that would help. Gave him a few tips to help him feel better and lit him a candle.

When someone is suicidal or obsessed with their own death (or the death of other people) they are in a bad mental state.

Cognitive Behaviour Technique or CBT and Meditation help.

Counselling, Homeopathy, Massage are also helpful.

Massage can really help as mental complaints are caused by spending too much time thinking and 'being' in the mind. Bringing someone back into their body when they're into thinking somersaults helps ground them.

Eating healthy foods, avoiding chemicals of any sort, especially recreational drugs, alcohol and coffee all of which cause far too much negative 'group thought' will balance things out a bit.

Deep studying, especially at University can bring all sorts of mental problems if there are no healthy-body-breaks, exercise or just walking in nature. I've treated Homeopathically numerous students in their final year/s when all that thinking has gone over the edge.

After Battling Demons

This gentleman has progressed really well on his path and his self-awareness is commendable.

My name is Andrew and I am 22 years old. I am writing to you because after reading the criteria for Indigo Children I realize that I am one (now a young adult). I've been through many hardships but after battling my demons I am now trying to live a healthy and spiritual life. I'm very interested in finding ways to improve myself and to deal with other people. I just wanted to send you my chart to see what you think. Thank you so much,

What I would ask would be 'what is it about other people that you need to deal with?' as people don't like to be 'dealt' with, they like to be treated equally. It makes me think of that classic fairy story, the 'Water-babies' by Charles Kingsley where there are two fairies one called Mrs Doasyouwouldbedoneby and the other called Mrs

Bedonebyasyoudid. The point he made in his book was you will receive what you give out.

Life Purpose

As this is such a common request from Indigos, I have dedicated a whole section of this book to the request. See Chapter 4.

"I recently read your post on the indigo people's links with astrological chart data. - in bundles etc. I am 100% sure that I am an Indigo, but am also hoping if you could be so kind to confirm it. I have almost all the traits and yearnings of an indigo, and I need to find my purpose in life to stabilize. I am hoping you can help.

I have attached a copy of my birth chart. Yours faithfully, Marani"

Sometimes when people find out that they are Indigo, for some strange reason, it makes them feel even *more* different and consequently, even *more* alone.

Michaela lives in the USA:

"I need a little help. I know I am a little late to bloom but I have gifts I must share and I feel like my light is fading. I feel tired always and feel like my body is becoming drained. I am withering. I have been prone to depression before. I help people all the time and another part of my soul's mission is to be a guide for my child. He is brilliant intuitive, gifted and very empathetic. I am afraid that if something were to happen to me, he may become like his father, abusive, destructive and detached from his feelings because he would be only exposed to invalidation if I were gone and his father and grandmother were raising him.

I originally found you because I was curious about how my chart seems so one sided and was wondering if that is why I feel sometimes like others can not see me or understand me. I feel like all they see is their reflection back and they take things out on me. I am trying my best to not personalize this. Although at this time I feel like many people come at me like authority figures and despise that I feel no sense of there being authority or hierarchy and they seem to want to make me see it their way or my fearlessness of and even love of my vulnerability. I would like to be able to protect myself and my child better. It seems very, very crucial. Thank you so very much,"

Monumental Truth

Sometimes the emails I receive are a bit more optimistic. Here's Rad a 20 year old in California:

"It's nice to know that there are some people out there who aren't indigos, but are trying to help us all the same. I'm also curious if you know approximately how common our births are or if there are many of us out there, because I was starting to feel quite alone discovering this monumental truth."

As you can grasp from this quote, discovering that you are an Indigo is a revelation and can seem a heavy responsibility.

Thinking goes along the lines of:

"Goodness me, I'm part of a chosen race, here to save the world spiritually! Crickey! How am I going to fulfill this heavy destiny? What will I have to change in my life to live up to this new life purpose? What will I have to do differently? Will I have to stop:

Drinking

Partying?

Taking occasional stimulants/drugs?

Smoking?

If we remember that most of life's problems are caused by the way we *think,* not what we *do* life takes on a less stressful appearance.

We are after all human beings, not human doings....

Some Indigos have a deep understanding and awareness of themselves. This can manifest as visions, intuition or dreams.

Cosmo is a Leo with Moon in Virgo and like many Indigos he has had lots of weird and wonderful experiences. Here is an example of just one of them. (He had a number of them while growing-up)

The Call, the Answer and Infinite Protector

'I had a vision I was lying in bed in my room facing the wall. I felt this oppressive malevolent force come over me it was suffocating. I felt so heavy and found it hard to move. Voices began to taunt me with harsh words that were untrue. It knew my weaknesses and was trying to use them against me so I would relinquish all hope. I tried to stand but I fell to my knees. I wanted to call out for help but was frozen with fear. I was afraid I would be attacked or it would take my life if I tried. Then a light appeared. I could feel a warm comforting presence coming from the light's source. I could feel it trying to reassure and prompt me to ask for help, but I was still too afraid to speak.

I felt guilty because my fear of the malevolent force was greater than my trust in the benevolent coming from the light. I tried many times to will myself to speak even if it was not that loud, but still nothing came out. I was upset, buried my head in my arms and began to cry. My mind spoke and said: "I'm sorry, I just can't."

Then it called out to me that it was the benevolent force and that it was loving and empathetic. It said – "Say it. All you need to do is ask me, ask me for help and I promise I will come."

It told me everything would be alright, but I had to trust that it would protect me and take the risk of asking it for help, as it could not intervene any further until I did so.

It could feel my fear and torment. It felt so sad like a loving and concerned parent. I could feel how badly it wanted to intervene and just take me away with or without me asking it. But for some reason it could not.

The energy was divine I believe it was the living universe.

I woke at 3:30am.'

This experience is 'divine' in that Cosmos was talking to and connected to a higher consciousness. Notice how he struggles with asking for help, while knowing that the benevolent force would help him. We fear loss more than benefit...

Think Differently About Suffering

The biggest piece of advice I can give anyone who is suffering, is to think differently about the suffering. For every negative thought there can also be a positive. In fact part of life's problems are caused by thinking too much. If we spent less time thinking and more time doing we feel better.

You know what it's like the more you think about something you don't like, the worse it gets. The Dalai Lama and Buddhists recommend an empty mind as a source of happiness and I agree with that.

Liberation from Thought

Without thought we are liberated.

I will give you an example.

Imagine that you go for a short walk, down a country lane through a few trees. As you're walking you could very easily spend your whole journey thinking about who said what, what you'd like to say, what you didn't say, what went wrong.... the lists can be endless.

What if you tackled it another way?

What if you had this short walk down a country lane and through a few trees and instead you *fully experienced everything* as it happens.

Do you hear the rustle of the tree's leaves?

Do you feel the hard baked earth underneath your shoes?

Do you see the different coloured flowers growing by the side of the path?

You could also experience the breeze that might be blowing through your hair.

Just spending 10 minutes in any given day, experiencing everything around you *as it happens* can liberate you from anxious or troubling thoughts.

An even easier version of this is to concentrate on your breathing.

Breath Counting

If you get stuck into a completely negative frame of mind, breathe in and out and as you breathe-count from 1 to 10.

Breathe in - 1

Breathe out -2

Breathe in -3

Breathe out - 4

.... And so on until you reach 10. Then when you get to 10 go back to 1 again and breathe in on the count of 1.

When things go Right

Sometimes, when life is going exactly as we want it to, something happens, that puts us back into a spin.

Help yourself by being less susceptible to burn-outs or break downs by being thankful for what you have, rather than moaning about what you haven't got.

Life isn't always, 24/7 horrible or nasty.

The trick, when you're younger, or even when you're older, is to avoid extremes of emotion. I don't mean don't be happy, but you'll be healthier if you don't go wild with happiness and rise to such a high that you bump your head on a cloud.

Moderation in all things.

'But', I hear you say, 'Life is Boring if it isn't Exciting.'

Life can be wonderful without speeding at 100 miles an hour. Life truly can be wonderful just by being....life.

Not every email I get is from an Indigo who is having a dreadful, horrible time. Sometimes they're very upbeat and happy!

Better Life

Here's an email from Candy born in 1993:

"My names Candy and I've been really searching myself the past couple months and have gotten deep into meditation. And just over the past couple months I've been following my gut and just going with everything I feel and life couldn't be better. I was also recently told that I might be an indigo by some friends, I was just wondering what my birth chart was like?"

Here's Rafa born in 1991:

"Hey I came across your website through Google. I am 22 years old from Israel,

I am an indigo without a doubt, I have wrote some of my thoughts regarding life when I was about 8 years old and my thoughts were not of an ordinary 8 year old boy,

My greatest joy comes from solving people's toughest problems, left school at the age of 15, successful today. I was wondering if you could confirm that for me with one of your charts.

Sometimes I find out what, underneath, are their true questions:

"My burning questions for now are.

1. What can I do to make this world a better place?

2. How can a person find their way in life and their purpose of life?

3. Why people in many cases do not appreciate kindness and good attitude of other person?"

The easiest way to solve that predicament is not to think about 'the world' as being some hard/awful/painful place full of greedy, nasty, horrible people. Aiming for the middle-ground of finding life does have ups and it does have downs, but it also has vast amounts of nothing and I think that's truly what people fear the most. That there is nothing

Nothing doesn't have to be fearful.

Quietness and Peace don't have to be boring.

We make the world a better place by enjoying the bit we're living in, giving some thanks for those things we have and working on the things we would like to have. Without complaining, blaming, or moaning.

We learned about life purpose in Chapter 4, so I won't repeat it here, but if you concentrate on 'being' not on 'doing' life gets shinier and happier.

Chapter 7

Self-Help Resources

Being independent minded might make you more likely to want to help yourself, which is the reason that I wrote this book.

Being able to help yourself is commendable, but keep in mind that if you are in a really bad space it is best to ask for help. This might seem difficult but in the long run it is better than your circumstances becoming so out of control that other people make decisions on your behalf.

Before you ask for help, get a piece of paper, or your journal and write down what help you would like.

Be specific

Keep this list available so you can refer to it every week and judge if you are actually getting the help you need.

Also if you are working out your own treatment programme, again write a short summary of what you want to have happen.

Don't put it in your phone or on your desktop or laptop or any electrical device.

Don't put it on your Facebook or Twitter and definitely don't 'share' what you are doing with your friends.

Problems get worse the more people you tell and can become magnified.

If you're using an on-line resource, I would recommend replace it with something face-to-face. It's hard to express how you feel on a computer.

If your life is a total mess, spend 20% - 30% of your time making it better otherwise you will wear yourself out.

You could devote 2 days a week to 'your problems and 5 days being a 'normal' person.

The trouble with self-help is it can eat up your time, so you're spending so much time trying to improve your 'self' your current life slips by.

Be sensible.

The sort of help you might need can be divided into:

Emotional help
Mental help
Physical help
Spiritual help

Emotional help

You might need emotional help when all you can do is cry, or you well-up when someone asks you how you are. Emotional problems include feeling tearful, feeling angry, sighing a lot, not wanting to be on your own, needing company, needing hugs and other tactile contact, or randomly sleeping with anyone and everyone you meet.

Keeping a journal and recording your feelings assists greatly when you are in a totally wobbly place. Writing every morning about the things that are upsetting you will allow you to get those feelings "off your chest".

Being able to talk to someone who has no personal relationship to you will also allow you to untangle these feelings in a counselling session.

Cut Out Coffee

One thing I'd definitely recommend to people that are overly emotional is to cut out coffee completely. Free yourself from the eternal ups and downs that coffee can bring. Start by drinking decaf for two weeks then on the third week have no coffee at all.

You will find by now, amazingly, your emotional ups and downs will have completely reduced.

However you might find that this seems boring and nothing is going on. Ignore that type of thinking, as it will only send you back to drinking coffee again and being up-and-down again.

For short-term relief use these Homeopathic remedies in a 6c or 30c potency

Ignatia for when you're sighing a lot, feeling tearful, getting angry with every little thing.

Natrum Muriaticum when your grief is deep-seated and from a hurt a long time ago

Pulsatilla when you're feeling really weepy and can't stop crying even though you are being comforted by someone.

You can take one tablet three times a day for a maximum of one week. If you still don't feel better, then seek out a Homeopath and go for a consultation.

Homeopathic Remedies are available from http://www.helios.co.uk/ or in the USA http://www.boironusa.com/wheretobuy/online/

Emotional Freedom Technique or EFT is another self-help technique that is really good for reducing stress. There are Acupuncture points on the body that you tap, whilst reciting aloud:

'Even though I feel...(sad, unhappy, cross with my boss, lonely) I deeply and completely love and accept myself.'

There are various websites that come and go with instructions but there is always a video on YouTube so search for EFT there and watch a demonstration.

Bach Flower Essences are also very good at helping emotional wobbliness.

The Twelve Healers fit nicely to the 12 signs of the Zodiac, so maybe choose one for your Sun sign, one for your Ascendant and one for your Moon.

Aries

Bach Flower Essence Impatiens:

'Those who are quick in thought and action and who wish all things to be done without hesitation or delay.'

Taurus

Bach Flower Essence Gentian :

'Those who are easily discouraged. They may be progressing well in the affairs of their daily life, but any small delay or hindrance to progress causes doubt and soon disheartens them"

Gemini

Bach Flower Essence Cerato:

'Those who have not sufficient confidence in themselves to make their own decisions'

Cancer

Bach Flower Essence Clematis:

'Living in the hopes of happier times, when their ideals may come true.'

Leo

Bach Flower Essence Vervain:

'Those with fixed principles and ideas, which they are confident are right'

Virgo

Bach Flower Essence Centuary:

'Their good nature leads them to do more than their own share of work and they may neglect their own mission in life.'

Libra

Bach Flower Essence Scleranthus:

'Those who suffer from being unable to decide between two things, first one seeming right then the other.'

Scorpio

Bach Flower Essence Chicory:

'They are continually correcting what they consider wrong and enjoy doing so.'

Sagittarius

Bach Flower Essence Agrimony:

'They hide their cares behind their humor and jesting and try to bear their trials with cheerfulness.'

Capricorn

Bach Fower Essence Mimulus:

'Fear of wordly things, illness, pain, accident, poverty, of dark, of being alone, of misfortune. They secretly bear their dread and do not speak freely of it to others'

Aquarius

Bach Flower Essence Water Violet:

'For those who like to be alone, very independant, capable and self-reliant. They are aloof and go their own way.'

Pisces

Bach Fower Essence Rock Rose:

'For cases where there even appears no hope or when the person is very frightened or terrified.'

Make this tri-ad of remedies up by putting two drops of each remedy in water and sipping throughout the day. Do this for a week and see how you feel. Again, if you're still feeling bad after a week, seek out help.

The organisations best suited to help in emotional circumstances are

UK

http://www.samaritans.org/

http://www.childline.org.uk/

http://www.youth2youth.org.uk/

Run by young people for young people

http://www.counselling-directory.org.uk/

http://www.itsgoodtotalk.org.uk/therapists/

USA

http://www.contact-usa.org/crisiscenters.html

http://www.samaritanshope.org/teen-helpline.html

Mental help

When your mental symptoms include irrational thoughts, having extreme highs and lows, feeling out of control, sleeplessness, great fear and anxiety and a disregard of your physical circumstances, you are in need of help.

You might be homeless, threatened with homelessness, out of work, or in a bad relationship.

Don't wait until you completely lose the plot, because someone is likely to alert the authorities and worst-case scenario you are sectioned and admitted to a mental health treatment centre.

Before you seek help make a note of what is worrying you the most and on a piece of paper write what you'd like to have happen, not your fears.

You might write something like "I would like my Obsessive Compulsive Disorder to be less of a worry."

Or you might write: "I would like to stop thinking about scary things like dying."

Most Indigos when they have a problem are likely to ask their friends for advice but this is the one time when your friends, unless they work in psychiatric care are unlikely to be able to help you.

The reason is, they have no experience of mental problems and while their help might be well intentioned, they've never been with someone or seen how things can progress or equally how things *can* improve with the right help.

You wouldn't expect your friends to understand bunging jumping if they'd never done it before, so don't expect them to understand mental health problems.

The sort of help you need is from someone experienced in mental health issues.

If you are already on a treatment program and are not happy with your care, get in touch with the organisations listed and see if you can get a second opinion.

In my opinion some drugs are worse than the problems they are supposed to solve. If the side-effects of drugs that you are already on are affecting your day-to-day existence, this is the time to have a review.

In the UK the help offered to people with mental health issues is extremely mixed, complex and founded on issues of control and authority. These obviously are not helpful foundations to assist an Indigo.

You are better off seeking help from a self-help group and there are a number run by Mind.

UK

http://www.mind.org.uk/help/mind_in_your_area

http://www.sane.org.uk/

USA

http://www.mentalhealthamerica.net/go/find_support_group

On-line self-help groups are counterintuitive and will only further drag you into the mental problems you have already.

Chemical Poisoning

You might find that your whole life needs a total review. You might need to reduce or cut out stimulants, coffee, alcohol, cigarettes or other forms of chemical poisoning.

The way of life advocated by Rudolf Steiner is the way to go.

He founded a form of healthy life-style that supports the person, and the planet called Anthroposophy.

UK http://www.anthroposophy.org.uk/

USA http://www.anthroposophy.org/

They have doctors trained in Homeopathy and gentle forms of treatment and if you can find yourself an Anthroposophic doctor you're less likely to be offered hard drugs.

UK https://www.anthroposophicmedicine.org.uk/

USA https://paam.wildapricot.org/

I'm not suggesting that you become a total hippie and live in a yurt, but spending more time in the quiet, or in beautiful solitary places will give your thoughts a chance to calm down.

If you would like Homeopathic treatment, and you live in the UK you can get an appointment on the NHS by asking your GP for a referral to one of the remaining Homeopathic Hospitals which are based in London and Glasgow

https://www.britishhomeopathic.org/treatment/nhs-homeopathic-treatment/

In the UK Homeopathy is divided into private treatments by practitioners trained in Homeopathy (like me) or doctors who are trained in medicine and then practice in the NHS.

UK practitioners can register with various organisations but there is no one place for all of them but this site lists some helpful info:

http://www.findahomeopath.org.uk/

Or you could search for one with the Federation of Holistic Therapists. I'm a member of this organisation and you can search on their website here

http://findatherapist.fht.org.uk/

This UK charity has useful information http://www.homeopathyactiontrust.org/

Worldwide info http://nationalcenterforhomeopathy.org/

Europe http://www.homeopathy-ecch.org/

Switzerland http://liga.iwmh.net/

Homeopathic Mental Stress Remedies

The Homeopathic remedies that will help with mental stress are:

Aconite (also called Aconitum Napellus) for fear, anxiety and/or physical and mental restlessness, fright

Argentum Nitricum for fear, anxiety and/or apprehension regarding future events.

Arsenicum Album for great anguish and feeling restless

Aurum Metallicum for deep gloom and despair and wanting to commit suicide

Ignatia for mental stress and strain from shock, bereavement and fright

Nux Vomica for feeling extremely irritable, fiery temperament and/or impatient

Phosphorous for feeling extremely sensitive, fearing being alone, of thunderstorms, fear of the dark, disease and death

You can take one tablet three times a day for a maximum of one week. If you still don't feel better, then seek out a Homeopath and go for a consultation.

Homeopathic Remedies are available from http://www.helios.co.uk/ or in the USA http://www.boironusa.com/wheretobuy/online/

The Bach flower remedies to help with anxiety's are listed on the Bach website here

http://www.bachcentre.com/centre/remedies.htm

EFT can help with low-level mental health issues.

You could tap on 'Even though I have (scary thoughts, lack of sleep, mixed thinking, lack of concentration) ... I deeply and completely love and accept myself.'

Like I have suggested in the emotional section, if you don't feel even a teeny bit better after a week, make an appointment to see a Homeopath, or counsellor.

If you are already on medication for anxiety, OCD, Attention Deficit Disorder (ADD) or Attention Deficit Hyperactivity Disorder (ADHD), find an alternative therapist you can trust and start working on your thoughts while agreeing a reduction in your medication. Don't just suddenly stop your drugs, take your time and work with your therapist.

Be sensible.

Be safe

Physical help

Physical help can include needing money, needing a job, needing somewhere to live, or needing transport to get to work.

Most people are happy to help in these types of circumstances, more so than offering mental or emotional help. However sleeping on a friend's living room floor for any length of time will strain a friendship and might cause you to flip into other areas of stress.

If you are already in work don't be in a rush to change the job until you have a clear idea of what you would prefer to do. It's far better to put up with a rubbishy job that pays the rent, than to lapse into unemployment. It is easier to go from one job to another than it is to go into work from unemployment.

Having said that if you are already unemployed find a charity, any charity whose ideals you agree with and volunteer for them until you find full-time work.

Everyone, millionaire or not, thinks they are not earning enough money!

If you have enough money to pay the rent and feed yourself when you're on track to being able to improve things. Instead of telling yourself how much you cannot afford, be realistic and work out what you can afford. Also it's very helpful to completely reassess your finances.

Money Record

One exercise that brings home how you spend your money is to record for exactly 4 weeks what you spend your money on. I do this every now and again and have done since I thought I wasn't earning enough money.

Get a teeny notebook and record in there (not on your iPhone, you need real paper!) exactly what you are spending your money on.

If you buy a magazine for £3.50, write that down.

If you buy a latte and a chicken wrap costing 10 Euros write that down.

If you spend $5 on bus fares, write that down.

The first time I did this exercise I realised I was spending 4% of my total salary on cappuccinos, something that was not helping my health, my bank balance, or my emotional well-being!

I'm not saying that you shouldn't spend some of your money on treats. What I am saying is be aware of, exactly aware, of where your money goes.

The amount of people that say to me "I don't know where my money goes", as if a bad–money–fairy was stealing their extra income overnight! It makes me wonder if they have ever tried this exercise. I then recommend it and they become liberated in their attitude towards their finances.

If you a homeless these organisations should help. Don't feel bad about asking for help, if they didn't have anybody needing their help, they'd go out of business!

International Homeless Help for Young People

http://www.depaulinternational.org/

UK Help

http://www.shelter.org.uk/

http://www.homelessuk.org/

For single homeless people

http://www.crisis.org.uk/

Homeless in London

http://www.mungos.org/

Homeless and Young in Surrey and Hampshire

http://www.stepbystep.org.uk/

If you're in financial difficulties these people will let you know what benefits you're entitled to and other support

http://www.turn2us.org.uk/

If you have a degree or a professional qualification these people provide help

http://www.elizabethfinncare.org.uk/

If you're under 18 and need help because of cruelty, there is info for adults too

http://www.nspcc.org.uk/

UK Self-help for all sorts of money issues

http://www.moneysavingexpert.com/

Homeless help in USA

http://www.salvationarmyusa.org/

Help with food and housing

http://www.211.org/

Government Housing and Homeless Local Assistance

http://portal.hud.gov/hudportal/HUD?src=/topics/homelessness/localassist

https://www.onecpd.info/homelessness-assistance/

Government Financial Assistance

http://www.usa.gov/Citizen/Topics/Benefits.shtml

Homeless Shelters

http://www.homelessshelterdirectory.org/

Spiritual help

Spiritual help might include wanting to know your true soul's path. I hope chapter 5 has helped you a little with this.

Astrology is beautifully designed to help in these situations. Due to its ancient roots and philosophical leanings, plenty of astrologers have debated and analysed the question "why am I here?"

Unlike religion, astrology offers *more than one path* to Nirvana. There are no codes or dogmas or regulations or expectations. You *can* find your true path in life by working on and understanding your North node and your Jupiter placement.

Before you investigate your North node it is better to have an understanding of astrology basics.

You can learn all you need to know in my easy-to-understand E-Book **6 Easy Steps in Astrology**

There is no shortage of organisations that will help you with your spiritual development. However you need to find a method that you feel happy and comfortable with. Try not to think of your spiritual path as located somewhere in the distant future. A lot of times when I'm reading for clients we discover they already are on their path, they just haven't realised it.

I would ask the question what does your Nirvana look like?

What does it feel like?

How different will it be to how things are now?

If we put to one side all the problems that you might be having. If we stop focusing on all the things that are going wrong. If we remember and appreciate the good things that we have already, Nirvana already exists. We haven't embraced it yet.

If you don't have any beliefs and think no religion can possibly help you, then contact these organisations. Keeping in mind what Indigo Vadim Zealand has said about pendulums, and that organisations in themselves feed on their members.

The Freedom from Religion Foundation

USA http://ffrf.org/

Humanist

UK https://humanism.org.uk/

USA http://americanhumanist.org/

Astrological Associations

UK http://www.astrologicalassociation.com/

USA http://www.astrologers.com/

Religious organisations

Buddhism

UK http://www.thebuddhistsociety.org/

Network of Buddhist Organizations http://www.nbo.org.uk/

USA http://www.baus.org/en/

Catholics

http://www.vatican.va/

Hindu

UK http://www.hinducounciluk.org/

USA http://www.hafsite.org/

Islam

UK http://www.mcb.org.uk/

USA http://iamc.com/

Jewish

UK http://www.masorti.org.uk/

USA http://www.jewishfederations.org/

Pagan

UK http://paganfed.org/

USA http://us.paganfederation.org/index.php

Protestant

http://www.churchofengland.org/

Sikh

UK http://www.sikhfederation.com/

USA http://www.sikhfoundation.org/

I have also written a book for each sign of the Zodiac, published by John Hunt Publishing

https://www.johnhuntpublishing.com/moon-books/authors/mary-english

I hope you have benefited from reading this book and feel a little clearer about your Life Path.

It would be lovely if you would write me a review from wherever you purchased this book.

If you'd like to learn Astrology (free) please go to my podcast http://astromary.libsyn.com/ and start at Episode One

If you need to book a personal one-to-one with me, please visit my website http://www.maryenglish.com

I am sending you heartfelt, kind and generous energies on your path and wish you all Good Things in Your Life:)

In Peace

Mary

xx

References

1. The Astrologers and their Creed by Christopher McIntosh, 1971, Arrow books, London.

2. p41, The Dawn of Astrology, 2008, Nicholas Campion, Continuum Books, London SE1 7NX

3/9 Jupiter An Astrologer's Guide, Eve Jackson, 1986, Sterling Pub Co Inc

4.The Gods of Change, Pain Crisis and the Transits of Uranus, Neptune and Pluto, by Howard Sasportas , Published 1989, Arkana, Penguin, London W8, England.

5. Understanding Your Life Thru Color, Nancy Ann (Tappe), 1986 Starling Publishers, PO Box 2697, Costa Mesa Ca 92626-2697. ISBN 0-940399-00-8 (Originally published as Enhancing Your Life Thru Color, 1982)

6. Indigos, The Quiet Storm, created by Nancy Tappe, written by Kathy Altaras, 2011, Aquila Media Productions, PO Box, 2884, Addison, TX 75001, ISBN 978-0-9822705-2-3

7. Cosmos and Psyche, Intimations of a New World View, Richard Tarnas, 2007, Plume, Penguin Group, 375 Hudson Street, New York, USA, ISBN 978-0-452-28859-1

8.The Guide to Horoscope Interpretation, Marc Edmund Jones, 1975, A Quest Book, published by The Theosophical Publishing House, Wheaton, Ill, USA, ISBN 0-8356-0442-x

The Care and Feeding of Indigo Children, Doreen Virtue, 2001, Hay House Inc, CA, USA, ISBN 978-1-56170-846-8

The Indigo Children, Essential Reading for All Parents of Unusually Bright and Active Children, Lee Carroll, Jan Tober, 1999, Hay House Inc, CA, USA, UK printing 2004, ISBN 1-56170-608-6

The Oxford Dictionary of Current English, 1991, Oxford University Press, Oxford, OX2 6DP, ISBN 0-19-281919-4

Homeopathic Remedies are available from http://www.helios.co.uk/ or in the USA http://www.boironusa.com/wheretobuy/online/

Don't miss out!

Visit the website below and you can sign up to receive emails whenever Mary English publishes a new book. There's no charge and no obligation.

https://books2read.com/r/B-A-WODI-NCTY

BOOKS 2 READ

Connecting independent readers to independent writers.

Also by Mary English

The Astrology of Lovers, How Astrology Can Help You Love Better
The Astrology of Indigos, Everyday Solutions to Spiritual Difficulties

Ingram Content Group UK Ltd.
Milton Keynes UK
UKHW042205080323
418239UK00001B/128

9 781393 655954